IMAGES
of America

NORWALK

Nathan Hale left a secluded cove in Norwalk on a mission to spy on the British in Brooklyn, New York. Designed by McKim, Mead and White, the Nathan Hale Memorial Fountain was dedicated by the Daughters of the American Revolution in 1901 in front of the Norwalk Armory on West Avenue. One side of it has a horse trough, and the other has a drinking fountain with a metal cup and dog bowls at the base. By the late 1920s, only the tablet was reassembled at Mill Hill after Armory Hill was widened. Later, that part was relocated to Nathan Hale Middle School, where it currently sits in disrepair. The author facilitated the return of the two-ton pink granite horse trough from Wilton (where it mysteriously sat at Ambler Farm for over 80 years) back to Norwalk. It will be restored and reerected as a fountain centerpiece in the community herb garden at Fodor Farm, which is along the trail that Hale traveled through Norwalk in 1776. (Author's collection.)

ON THE COVER: A smartly attired group enjoys a sail in the Norwalk Harbor in the summer of 1908. (Author's collection.)

IMAGES
of America

NORWALK

Lisa Wilson Grant

ARCADIA
PUBLISHING

Published by Arcadia Publishing
Charleston, South Carolina

Library of Congress Control Number: 2013946733

For all general information, please contact Arcadia Publishing:
Telephone 843-853-2070
Fax 843-853-0044
E-mail sales@arcadiapublishing.com
For customer service and orders:
Toll-Free 1-888-313-2665

Visit us on the Internet at www.arcadiapublishing.com

To my father, Donald Wilson, whose dedication to this community began in the early 1960s as a Norwalk Public Schools math teacher. He continues to be my source of inspiration.

CONTENTS

ACKNOWLEDGMENTS

Like a crazy quilt, Norwalk is diverse and varied in both its people and the distinct areas in which people live. It is impossible to include everyone who has ever lived or worked here or include vintage photographs of all the buildings that ever existed in the space allowed for this book. I have separated the various parts of Norwalk into chapters and have included the images of what I've found to be noteworthy within those areas. Unless they were particularly interesting, I have tried not to include photographs used in other books about Norwalk. Having grown up in the 1960s and 1970s, I've also included places that fascinated me then as they do now—places like Old MacDonald's Farm where I had birthday parties and Louie's in Rowayton where I rode my bike to purchase candy and gum. There are so many people who helped me with this project, and I'd like to thank the following, including many others in the Norwalk Facebook groups who contributed many tidbits on Norwalk history. Thank you, to all who provided information or photographs to me: Robin Axness, Doug Bora Sr., the Canevari family, Paul and Elaine Deysenroth, Peter Albin Deysenroth, Carol Ann Falasca, Karen Fecenko-Lyon, the Fodor family, Leigh Finlay, Joel Flora, Lloyd Rex Gatten, the Gavrielidis family, Susan Gilgore, Jordan Grant, Ben Guerrero, Rachael Guest, Steve Haywood, Marianne Josem, Paul Keroack, Kathleen Kiska, Lesley Korzennik, Don LaJoie, Maggie Levy, Mary Ellen McDonald, George Middleton, Irwin Miller, Mike Mocciae, Nancy Moore, George Nemeth Jr., Margo Melton Nutt, Lou Renzuella, Steve Rudolf, Bob Russell, Joseph Ruta, Larry Scharbach, Vinny Scicchitano, Michael Shaffer, David Smith, Walter Stelkovics, Stew Leonard's, Pam Vincent, Laurie Weinstein, and Charles Yost. Special thanks go to Ralph Bloom, Peter Bondi, Tod Bryant, John Kurtzman, Dana Laird, and Wendell Livingston for reading through the final version of the manuscript and sharing their knowledge of Norwalk history.

All images that do not have a credit are from the collection of the author. Daughters of the American Revolution is abbreviated as DAR.

INTRODUCTION

In the 16th century, Native Americans inhabited the area we now call Norwalk. These Indians were part of a unique tribe that belonged to a larger group called the Lenape or Delaware Indians, and they spoke a Munsee dialect. They were hunters and gatherers in the fields and forests, they caught fish and shellfish, and they grew corn, pumpkins, and squash. They made jewelry and wampum out of shells. To protect themselves from the Pequots, they would build tall forts, such as the palisade fence that was located in the Fort Point Street area in East Norwalk.

In 1497, England first claimed property discovered by Sebastian Cabot, and after England saw how successful the Pilgrims were in Plymouth Colony, many Puritans arrived in the Massachusetts Bay Colony eager to set up new towns. The Great Migration started in the 1630s, and the good lands in eastern Massachusetts quickly became exhausted. After the Pequot War in 1637, three competing English land companies (Connecticut Colony, New Haven Colony, and Massachusetts Bay Colony) sought to quickly purchase land in western Connecticut to accommodate this wave of new immigrants before the Dutch settlers moved eastward from New Amsterdam.

In February 1640, Roger Ludlow from the Connecticut Colony purchased land on the eastern side between the Saugatuck and Norwalk Rivers for trade goods from the "Indians of Norwake," and he himself settled in Fairfield. He was later twice reprimanded by the General Court of Connecticut for founding the settlement in Fairfield instead of the area that is now Bridgeport where he was ordered to and for taking up arms against the Dutch on a matter with the Indians with which the court disagreed. Disgraced, he moved to Virginia and then back to England.

Capt. Daniel Partrick made the deal in April 1640 with sachem Mahachemo and purchased the lands between the Norwalk River and the Five Mile River. He later moved on to Greenwich, where he met with a violent death a few years later in Stamford by Dutchmen who accused him of treachery with the Indians.

In 1651, Richard Olmstead and Nathaniel Ely signed a treaty with Runkinheage, Piamikin, and others for the western part of Norwalk. This treaty caused controversy over the Norwalk-Stamford line, which was established in a 1643 treaty with Andrew Ward and Richard Law of Stamford. Piamikin, the sagamore of the Roatons, had signed both agreements for the same land. The disagreements went on for years until finally, in 1673, the general court intervened and determined that Five Mile River was to be the boundary line as per the earlier agreement.

The first Norwalkers settled in the East Norwalk area, where the first home lots were drawn. East Avenue was the "Towne Street," and the town quickly expanded to the Wall Street area, with the Norwalk Green as the center. The original area of Norwalk included rural areas where "out-livers" formed parishes as they lived a distance from the church in the center of Norwalk. The roads were mainly based on Indian trails. The Norwalk area included half of New Canaan (which was Canaan Parish), Saugatuck, Wilton (which was Wilton Parish), and Lewisboro, New York.

On July 11, 1779, the Battle of Norwalk became the largest Revolutionary War battle in Connecticut. Earlier, Nathan Hale, an American spy, had set out from Norwalk on an ill-fated mission. Twenty-six hundred British and Hessian troops landed at Calf Pasture. The British set homes on fire at Washington and Water Streets and up Flax Hill. They burned more houses as they marched down West Avenue and Wall Street. This was followed by raids along the local coves, taking not only livestock and household goods but also captives for prisoner exchanges.

Many mills were erected on Norwalk's rivers—sawmills, gristmills, and wool and cotton mills. The Winnipauk area developed around the mills, and Silvermine had several, too. Broad River, West Norwalk, and Cranbury were farming districts. Rowayton was a center of a prosperous oyster business on the Five Mile River. Oyster houses also lined the Norwalk Harbor, and by 1880, Norwalk had the largest fleet of steam-powered boats in the world.

Old Well was a hamlet across the Norwalk Harbor that increased in population with the transition of transportation from the sailing ships in the earlier days to steamships. Renamed South Norwalk, the city really grew when the New York & New Haven Railroad came through in 1849. The Danbury & Norwalk Railroad connected the two towns in 1852.

There were seven Norwalk potteries through the years and at one time over 45 hat manufacturers, which provided ample employment for the influx of people moving in.

Norwalk and South Norwalk grew as very distinct, separate cities. Norwalk was "uptown" and South Norwalk was "downtown" and there was a lot of antagonism between the two. The reason for this may be that South Norwalk was an area of newcomers, immigrants who were eager to work in a new country, as opposed to Norwalkers, who had deep roots here and attended churches of similar faith. Catholics first met in residences as early as 1828, though St. Mary's Chapel was not erected in Norwalk until 1851 and St. Joseph's Parish in South Norwalk in 1895. Consolidation of the two cities took place in 1913, but it was reluctantly done in the opinion of many of the residents at the time.

In the 1800s, industrialization started to take place—large factories manufacturing goods such as firearms, buttons, shoes, cloth, and hats were increasing in Connecticut and in Norwalk. Workers came up from Chesapeake, Maryland, to work as oystermen. Wealthy owners and managers of businesses lived on Golden Hill overlooking South Norwalk. Immigrants came into Norwalk from many places. One of the largest groups to come here in the early 1900s was the Hungarians; there were also many Eastern European Jews and Italians, among others.

The Ku Klux Klan made a nationwide resurgence in the early 1920s; there was a Klavern here in Norwalk as well as other surrounding towns. There were meetings held at Highland Park off Flax Hill Road. In the summer of 1923, Klan members set fire to a 30-foot-tall cross at Calf Pasture Beach and painted a large "KKK" on the stone wall surrounding James A. Farrell's estate in Rowayton. Their doctrine preached a suppression of blacks, Jews, and Catholics. Fortunately, it died out quickly in the area. There were also restrictive communities, such as Rowayton Beach Association, that screened new homeowners before they could buy a home to live there and had a guard stationed to keep "outsiders" from coming in or using the private beach. Today, it is hard to imagine these practices.

On the other hand, there are stories of people not feeling discriminated against, such as the Sasaki family that owned the Owl restaurant in 1941, when Japanese forces attacked Pearl Harbor. There were a lot of Norwalkers who made sure he reopened his business regardless of the Japanese resentments at the time.

Norwalk is a diverse population, and that is what makes it an interesting place to live. Although there are many sections of Norwalk and more taxing districts than most other cities, it continues to be a wonderful place to live and also to raise a family. There are beautiful beaches, art centers, historical events, and festivals, and with its proximity to New York, there's always something to do. Although for many years historic buildings were torn down, there are many now who see to the preservation of historic structures. My hope is for more people to become aware of our local history, so that there will be respect for the people and the architecture of the past.

One

IN AND AROUND
NORWALK

This wrought iron sign on the Norwalk & Darien town line on the Post Road (Connecticut Avenue) was designed by artist Alexander Rummler and features a silhouette of the Old Town House, which is the meetinghouse at Mill Hill, now the site of the Norwalk Historical Society. Norwalk was purchased in 1640 but not settled until 1651. (Courtesy of Ben Guerrero Collection.)

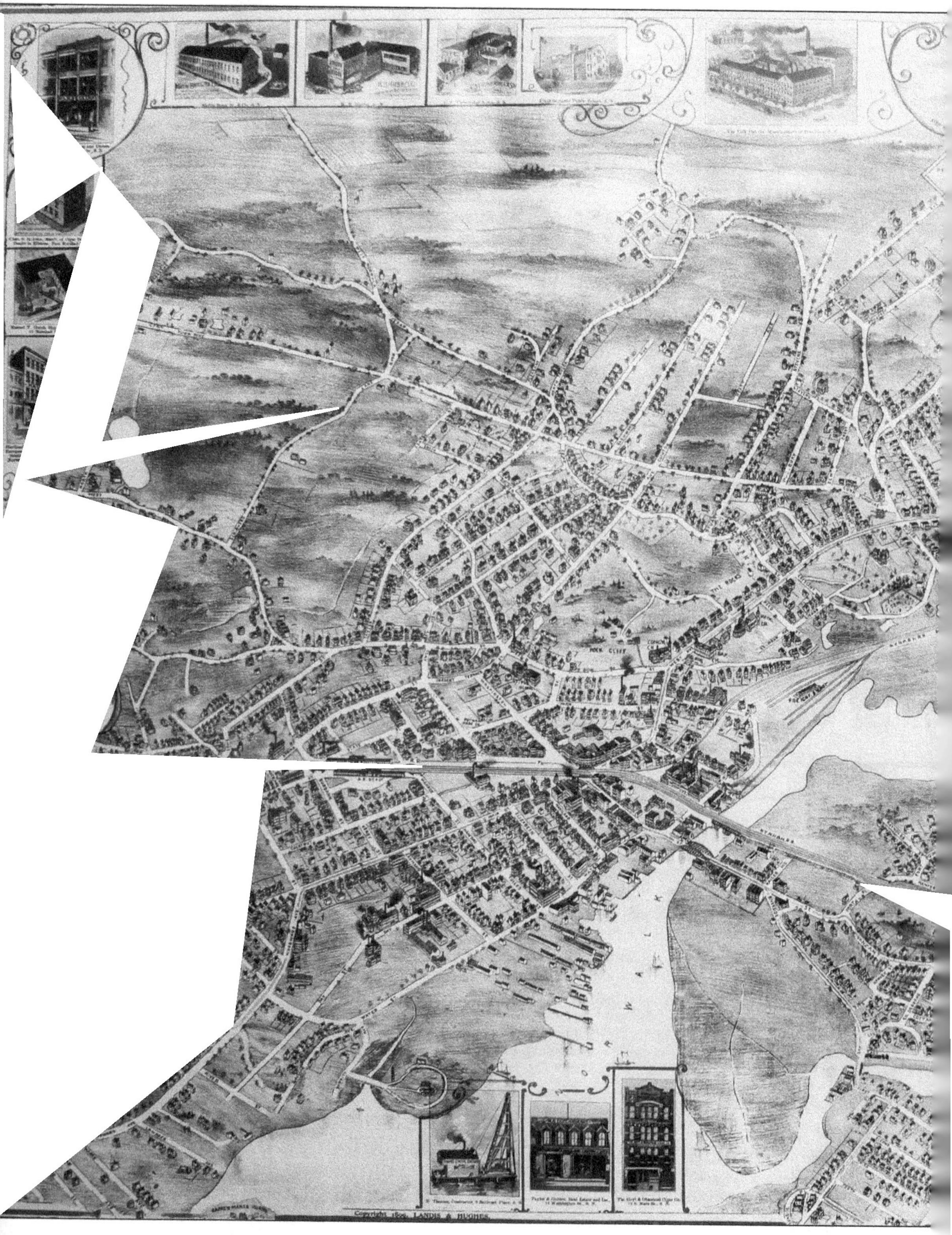
ROCK CLIFF
LANDIS & HUGHES

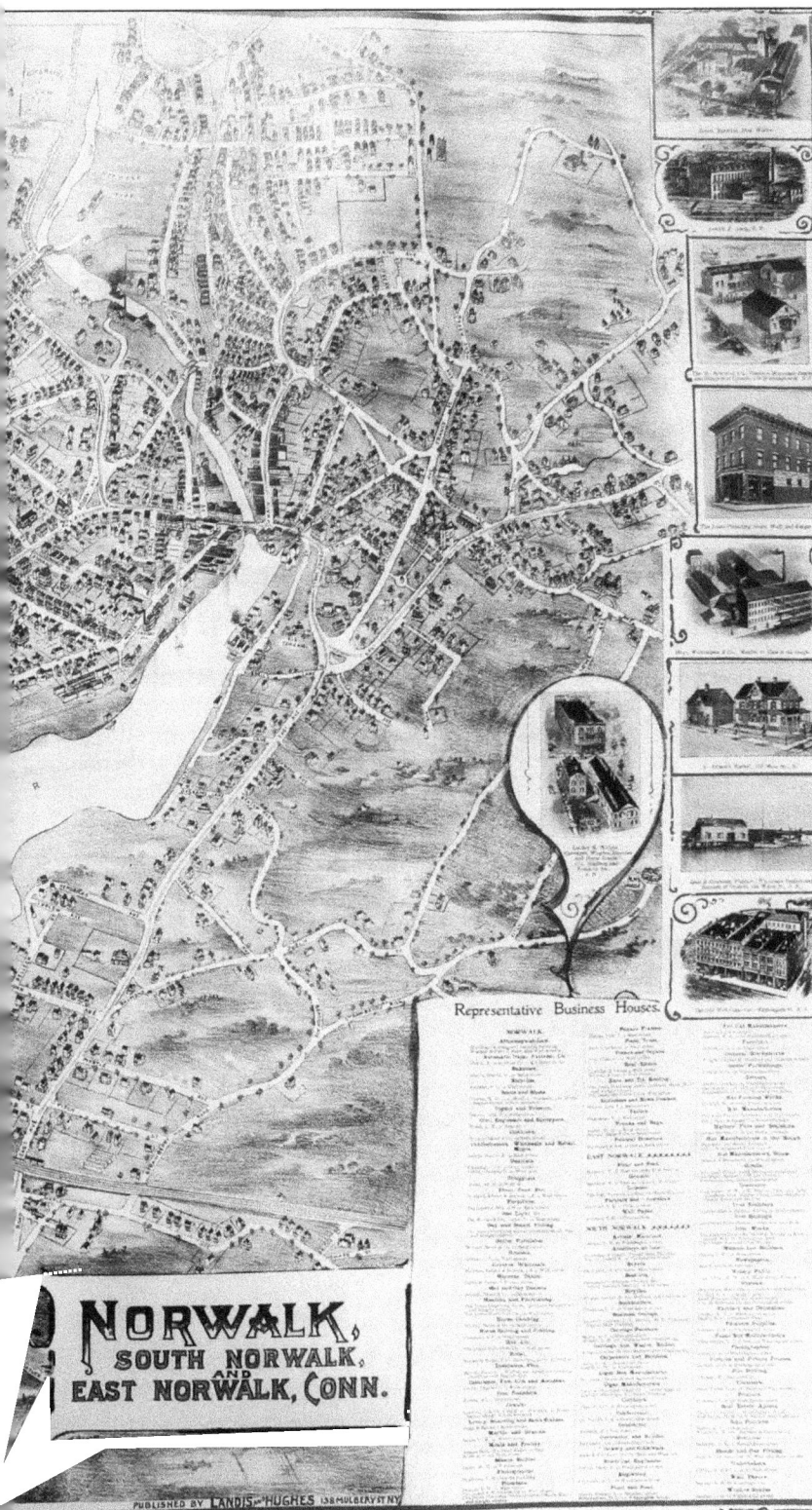

Representative Business Houses.

NORWALK, SOUTH NORWALK, AND EAST NORWALK, CONN.

PUBLISHED BY LANDIS & HUGHES 138 MULBERRY ST NY

This Landis and Hughes map of 1899 shows Norwalk, South Norwalk, and East Norwalk. Norwalk was chartered as a town on September 11, 1651, was reincorporated as a borough in 1836, and was reincorporated as a city in 1893. South Norwalk became a city in 1870. The consolidation of South Norwalk, Norwalk, and the East Norwalk Fire District occurred in 1913.

11

Under construction in this 1898 photograph, the First Methodist Church on West Avenue included the bell from the old church. The old building was floated down the harbor to Westport, where it was a barn for many years. This unique yellow-brick building was designed by noted church architect Melvin Hubbard. It contains beautiful stained glass, including the largest stained-glass window in a Connecticut church. One is of Jesse Lee, an early founder of Methodism in New England, who preached his first sermon under an apple tree in Norwalk in 1789. There is a plaque at Cross and Main Streets near that spot. (Courtesy of Peter Albin Deysenroth.)

WEST AVENUE, NORWALK, CONN.

West Avenue is the link between the South Norwalk area and the Wall Street area of Norwalk. In the 1840s, David Swords first established the horse-drawn omnibus wagon connecting the two. This was then put out of business by the Norwalk Horse Railway Company formed by LeGrand Lockwood, the third trolley in the state of Connecticut at the time. This photograph, taken many years later, shows established elms that have since disappeared.

Norwalk's first high school building was this yellow-brick one on West Avenue across from the Lockwood-Mathews Mansion. In 1938, students attended the new campus on East Avenue, which is now the Norwalk City Hall. Today, Norwalk High School's third home is on County Street.

Norwalk High School's 1914 baseball team is pictured here. Among those in the photograph are Nat Goodwin (second from left), whose clothing store of the same name carried "better men's suits" for decades, and Lou Tarlov (seventh from left), who continued to be active in sports, including working with youngsters in the recreation department. He was honored by the Norwalk Old Timer's Athletic Association in 1966. (Courtesy of the Jewish Historical Society of Fairfield County.)

Construction of LeGrand Lockwood's mansion is seen above around 1865. The stonemasons and woodworkers arrived on ships that transported rare woods and marble from Europe. These craftsmen lived in the outbuildings on the property during construction. A Second Empire country house, Elm Park was completed in 1868 and looked onto both the Norwalk Harbor and Lockwood's horse railroad on West Avenue. Lockwood lost his fortune in the Panic of 1873 and had to mortgage the house to J.P. Morgan to pay his business debts. In 1876, Charles D. Mathews purchased it as a summer residence. Below is the drawing room as it was when the Mathews family lived there. The Mathewses kept the home until 1938, when it passed to the city. Used primarily for office space and storage, it then fell into disrepair. In 1963, the city was determined to tear it down. Fortunately, a group of forward-thinking citizens tirelessly fought that idea, and ongoing restoration has continued ever since. Today, the Lockwood-Mathews Mansion Museum is a National Historic Landmark. (Both, courtesy of the Lockwood-Mathews Mansion Museum.)

The Norwalk Armory was located across the street from the Lockwood-Mathews Mansion and was removed when the Route 7 connector to I-95 was built. The Nathan Hale Fountain was in the road at front. The tablet on the back of the fountain was given by the children of Norwalk and reads, "I only regret that I have but one life to lose for my country."

The dances at the Norwalk Armory were very popular and had themes such as Washington's Birthday, as in this promotional photograph by Rudolf Hunziker.

When the Norwalk Hospital was first located on 24 Leonard Street in 1893, it contained separate wards for men and women. Pictured here is the hospital that was constructed in 1899 on Armory Hill on the Post Road. A school of nursing was added, and in 1918, a larger hospital was built on Stevens Street. A 1949 *Saturday Evening Post* cover by artist Stevan Dohanos features a mother and her newborn being discharged at the Norwalk Hospital.

The 1881 French cannon, presented to the city in 1921, once sat across from the library. The cannon was captured by German forces during World War I and recaptured by the French. Over the years, as the roads changed, the cannon and its base were separated. Fully restored in 2009, the cannon was painted gray and sits proudly together with its base on the Norwalk Green. Names of World War I soldiers are engraved in its base.

The Norwalk Public Library was the first Carnegie library in Connecticut. In 1903, it received a $20,000 grant from Andrew Carnegie. In addition to the grant, a generous donation of land, once occupied by the former Norwalk Lawn Tennis Club, made it possible to build this exquisite library at 1 Belden Avenue. The building still exists today, with a large addition that is in a more modern style. The English Elizabethan Revival building has symmetrical facades and columns flanking the front entrance.

Wall Street is pictured around 1900 with horse-drawn carriages and trolley tracks in the road. On the right is Tristam and Hyatt's dry goods store, which opened in 1891 at 28 Wall Street.

The Royal James Inn started out as a Greek Revival residence built by William Kellogg James in 1840. By 1920, it had been enlarged and converted into a hotel. The building was razed in 1929. Many of its exquisite Chinese antiques, mahogany dining table and lyre back chairs by New York cabinetmaker Duncan Phyfe, beautiful old costumes from 1750 to 1860, and rare Wedgwood bowls were bequeathed to the Metropolitan Museum of Art in New York City by Maria P. James in 1910.

A parade proceeds down Wall Street passing by many shoe stores and cigar shops in this c. 1900 photograph. According to Elsie Nicholas Danenberg's *Romance of Norwalk*, in 1850, there were 4,651 inhabitants, and "the boot and shoe industry . . . employed nearly 500 people and was [another large] manufacturing interest [in Norwalk] . . . at the time." (Courtesy of Peter Bondi.)

Baldwin's Express on 37 Wall Street still used horse transportation in 1895 to Bridgeport, with a stop also in Westport. The nearby trolley barn at 10 Wall Street was built in 1864. In 1895, horse-drawn trolleys gave way to electric trolleys, but in 1935, buses replaced trolleys altogether. (Courtesy of the Norwalk History Room at the Norwalk Public Library.)

The flood of 1955 was disastrous for the downtown Main and Wall Street areas. The 12-plus inches of rainfall caused foundations to be undermined. Many bridges along the Norwalk River were destroyed. Many buildings close to the river in the downtown area were never reconstructed, and the space was converted into a park. Freese Park is named after Norwalk's first Socialist mayor, Irving Freese. (Both, courtesy of Peter Bondi.)

Stores line the foot of Mill Hill at Wall Street around 1900. The shipping and general store of E. Lockwood and Sons was on the left. Brook Street, on the right, is now a parking lot. The narrow Lewis Way is a walkway up the hill towards Norwalk Green today. One of the oldest potteries, Norwalk Pottery Company, was located off to the left at 6 Smith Street. (Courtesy of the Norwalk History Room at the Norwalk Public Library.)

The area that intersects near Mill Hill and East Avenue once contained a rotary named Washington Circle. Today, traffic lights and separate lanes control the convergence of the same five streets. In the 1970s, the gazebo on the green was painstakingly replicated to match the old one, which it replaced. In 2013, the First Taxing District built a new bandstand that, although it deviates from the original structure, better fits today's needs in its larger size and design.

An 1855 engraving from *Ballou's Pictorial* of the Norwalk Green shows cows freely grazing. In the central background is St. Paul's Church, founded in 1737. The current church is the fifth structure erected on the site. The Congregational church is on the left-hand side; the original church was established in 1652 near the intersection of East Avenue and Fort Point Street. The green was shaded by notable elms in the late 1800s, but they unfortunately were ravaged by beetles.

Bicycle racers and spectators are gathered along the Norwalk Green in front of 7 Park Street, the former home of silversmith Levi Clark, around 1890. The green, along with its bandstand, has always been an important place for patriotic and other events, particularly for the beginning and ending of parades. (Courtesy of Michael Shaffer.)

This aerial view shows Norwalk High School on East Avenue. With enrollment bursting at the seams, Brien McMahon High School freshmen also used this building as an annex in the 1970s. It underwent a complete conversion from school to Norwalk City Hall, which is what it is today, and contains an extensive collection of Works Progress Administration (WPA) murals created during the Great Depression era located in the central halls of the building.

The Fairfield County Children's Home was on Westport Avenue, and in 1929, there were 400 children cared for there. Today, this area is across the street from what is now Stew Leonard's, a unique dairy farm–grocery store.

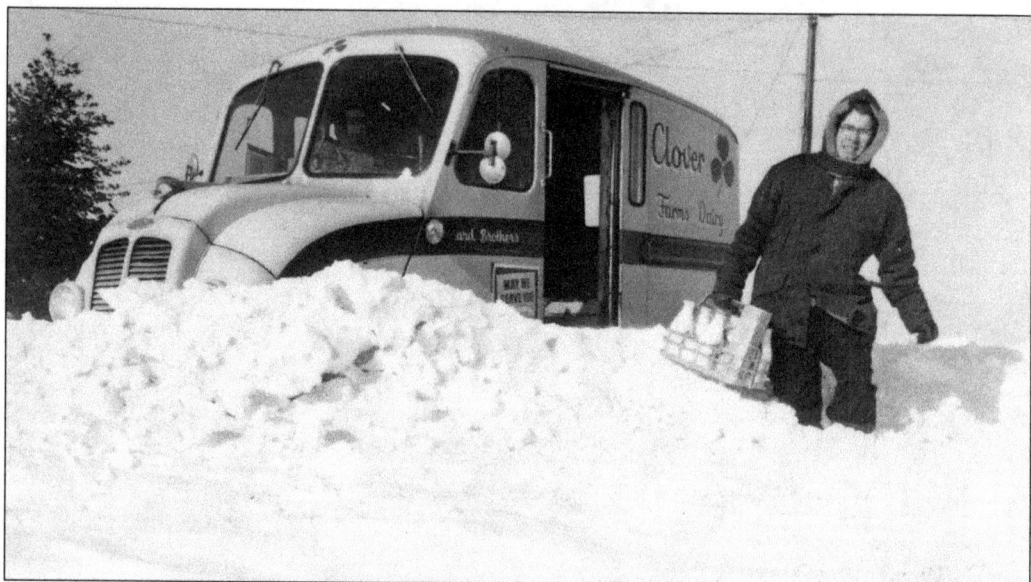

Clover Farms Dairy was started in 1921 by Charles Leo Leonard. His son, Stew Leonard, shown in this c. 1950 photograph delivering milk out of a Divco milk truck, inherited the Clover Farms milk delivery business. In 1971, the store was renamed Stew Leonard's. The family continues to be involved with the store today, which is proclaimed to be the world's largest dairy by *Ripley's Believe it Not!* (Courtesy of Stew Leonard's.)

Fred Murphy of the Crystal Ice Company built the original skating rink in 1940 next to his plant on Crescent Street. Leo Skidd took over in 1945 and ran it for the next 50 years. He added a roof in 1957. Crystal Ice Rink was home to the Norwalk Hockey Club and the Home Oil Hockey Club, which became the semiprofessional team Home Oilers. World-class figure skaters Dorothy Hamill and Carol Heiss rented ice time there for training. (Courtesy of the Norwalk History Room at the Norwalk Public Library.)

THE FAIRFIELD COUNTY DAIRY CO.
NORWALK, CONN.

Deliver _____ 191___
Quarts Milk
½ Pints Cream

Name
Address

The Fairfield County Dairy Company was on Grand View Avenue at the corner of Prospect Avenue in the Spring Hill area. Edward K. Austin was its president and treasurer from 1911 to 1913. He lived nearby on 8 Arch Street. This whole area is now reconfigured with the Route 7 connector to I-95.

The reference to a summit that is no longer there may seem odd—Grumman's Hill was removed by a developer in the 1920s. This marker is in proximity to that spot, which today is in front of the Norwalk Inn. Near here, Maj. Gen. William Tryon sat in a confiscated rocking chair and witnessed the burning of Norwalk by the British troops and Hessian mercenaries hired by the British during the American Revolution.

25

With two signs highlighting chicken and waffles, it seems that was a real hit at this restaurant on Westport Avenue. Although the building is still there today on the corner of Westport Avenue and Strawberry Hill, it is no longer a restaurant and has fewer glass windows.

In 1937, Margaret Rudkin lived in Fairfield, Connecticut, on a beautiful property called Pepperidge Farm. Her youngest son had severe allergies and asthma, which made him unable to eat most commercially processed foods. Instead of making the common white bread, Margaret decided to try her hand at baking him some all-natural stone-ground whole wheat bread with vitamins and nutrients intact, and that was the beginning of the bakery that is now a huge enterprise.

Squab is a young, domestic pigeon and apparently was quite the delicacy in the early 1900s, when the Royal Squab Company existed at 56 Newtown Avenue. Upon close examination, one can see the pigeons within the cages on this winter morning.

Joseph Loth and Company began producing ribbons, tie silks, and woven silk labels in Manhattan around 1875. Silk ribbons were used in the decoration of hats, clothing, and furnishings and could be dyed in rich colors and woven in intricate patterns. In 1896, Joseph Loth retired, and the business was continued by his two sons. His son Henry moved 100 narrow looms to this mill at 25 Grand Street in Norwalk. In 1985, the building was tastefully refurbished as loft-style apartments.

This panoramic photograph of the Center Junior High School class of 1945 was taken by Mrdich Manugian. In addition to his group shots such as this, Manugian took photographs for the *South Norwalk Sentinel*. His studio was located at 69 Flax Hill Road. Center Junior High School was located on Main Avenue. It was converted into board of education offices in the 1970s and later torn down to make way for new apartments. This building was the original location of six easel

paintings by Justin Gruelle that illustrate Mark Twain stories, and the mural *The Duke vs. The King*—also based on a Mark Twain story—by George Avison, created between 1935 and 1940 for the Works Progress Administration (WPA). All have been restored and are on display at Norwalk City Hall and Norwalk Community College.

The Norwalk Airport was located on West Rocks Road. There was a watchtower here during World War II from which air raid spotters identified airplanes flying overhead to Mitchel Field on Long Island. Dr. Alvin Wadsworth owned this property and left it to the Catholic Church. It was the site of Central Catholic High School from 1959 through 1989, after which it became All Saints Catholic School, which it remains today. (Courtesy of the Norwalk History Room at the Norwalk Public Library.)

The France Street tablet was erected by the DAR in 1894 to commemorate the American patriots who bravely fought at the Battle of the Rocks. Norwalk suffered more destruction during the Revolution than any other town in the state—130 homes, 40 shops, 100 barns, 2 churches, 4 mills, and 5 vessels and saltpans were destroyed. Years later, the government made restitution to the sufferers through grants of land in the Connecticut Western Reserve in Ohio, known as the "Firelands." (Photograph by the author.)

Two

Early Roots in
East Norwalk

In 1898, a large monument of Quincy granite was dedicated in East Norwalk bearing two bronze bas-relief tablets that feature Roger Ludlowe trading with the Indians. In this undated photograph, there is a large gathering in front of the Roger Ludlowe Monument with costumed "Indians" with Western-style headdresses on Gregory Boulevard, which was at one time was named Ludlow's Parkway and was the original cow path to the pasture. (Courtesy of the Norwalk History Room at the Norwalk Public Library.)

This map, drawn in 1847 by Edwin Hall, shows the early home lots located on either side of Towne Street, later East Avenue, in 1665. The oldest road in Norwalk is what is shown on this map as the Ancient Country Road from Stamford to Fairfield. It followed the Stamford Path on today's Flax Hill Road as the King's Highway to the west and Strawberry Hill Road to Fairfield in the other.

Sea View Avenue, South Norwalk, Conn.

213652

Above, a trolley is headed east on Sea View Avenue alongside beautiful Victorian homes up on the hill. The field to the left was once a landfill known as Duffy's Field and is now Veteran's Park, which contains a public boat ramp and ball fields and is home to many summer events, such as the Norwalk Oyster Festival, held each year on the weekend after Labor Day. Below, boats are moored in the water just around the bend on Seaview Avenue. The residence on the far right is now the Pastime Athletic and Social Club.

Sea View Ave., East Norwalk, Conn.

Canevari's grocery store was known to have the freshest vegetables around. It was located at 210 Washington Street, between Seaview Avenue on the right and Fort Point Street at left, where the two trolley cars are in this photograph. Fort Point was so named as it was the site of an old Indian fort with tall palisade walls in the 17th century. (Courtesy of the Canevari family.)

This 1910 photograph was taken from the East Norwalk side of the Washington Street bridge looking towards South Norwalk. A muzzled dog is sunning himself at Liberty Square. This wooden bridge, built in 1867, was deemed unsafe for public travel and was replaced in 1914 with a concrete bridge with a steel draw that was stronger and better equipped to handle the increase in trolley car traffic and the population, which at the time was 5,000 in East Norwalk and 11,000 in South Norwalk and growing. (Courtesy of Kathleen Kiska.)

Built right at the water's edge, Overton's is no stranger to coastal flooding, as evidenced in these 1940s photographs. The charming roadside stand still exists today, selling hot dogs, hamburgers, clam bellies, and more. Missing today are the glass windows on the sides. The building in the background (formerly the Penny Arcade building, which was floated there on a barge from Roton Point amusement park) was repurposed as the Sea View restaurant. Completely rebuilt, that same restaurant today is Harbor Lights. Below, the boat livery and bait shop building is today alongside the Overton's picnic table deck, where patrons can eat and enjoy a beautiful view of the Norwalk harbor—just don't start feeding the seagulls. (Both, courtesy of the Gavrielidis family.)

Crofut and Knapp Hat Factory was organized in 1858 by Andrew J. Crofut and James H. Knapp. Crofut was from Danbury and was an expert in the stiffening of felt hats using shellac. This was an important business move that produced the first derby hat in America and continued with new hat styles into the early 20th century. John B. Stetson, a Danbury hatter, learned his skills from Crofut and Knapp.

A Marvin Elementary School student named Clifford sent this postcard to wish the recipient well, and he also identifies himself as being in the photograph. Built in 1902, the brick former school building on 60 Gregory Boulevard is now a combination assisted living elderly housing and childcare facility known as the Marvin.

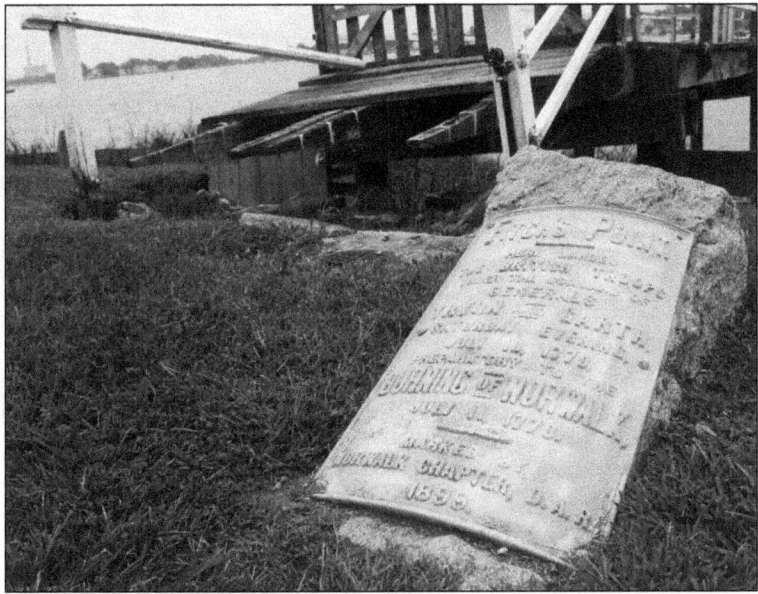

The monument at Fitch's Point is located near a dock on a private road along the Norwalk Harbor. It was erected by the DAR in 1899 and marks the place where British troops landed on July 10, 1779, before they burned Norwalk the next day. In the distance, the imposing Manresa Island power plant, an eyesore since the 1960s, ceased operations in 2013. (Photograph by the author.)

Charpentier Se Recommande Pour Vins, Liqueurs, Homards et Bonnes Viandes.

232 East Avenue, East Norwalk, Conn. Closed Mondays.
Tel. Norwalk 8-9903

Maybe it's the striped awning, perhaps it's the old automobiles, but the Charpentier Restaurant in this postcard somehow appears much more cheerful looking in this 1940s image than today. After 20 years of meat experience at the Cudahy Packing Company, Arthur M. Charpentier opened his own meat market in South Norwalk in 1925, moving just a year later to open this steak and lobster house at 232 East Avenue.

Norwalk Street Railway Company's open four-wheel trolley No. 11 is headed from the shore on West Avenue back to the South Norwalk train station. At the end of Gregory's Point, Dorlon's was a favorite resort in the summer and, according to a 1901 article in the *New England Magazine*, "a good hotel furnishing shore dinners and excellent bathing facilities [that] are the attractions of the place." In addition to the bathhouses, there was also a big picnic pavilion, horse sheds, and a dance hall. Earlier, in the middle of the 19th century, this property was a shipbuilding yard. It was enlarged, and a hotel was added. It was sold to Philetus Dorlon in 1874.

Dorlon's Point Hotel is pictured before the 1902 fire. Dorlon's was the site of the annual Fat Man's Club clambakes, of which owner Philetus Dorlon was the president. The men gorged themselves on clams, chickens, lobsters, corn on the cob, potatoes, sweet potatoes, and watermelons and weighed themselves afterwards. According to the September 17, 1885, *New York Times*, "The fat men filled with clams and sorrow, the sudden gloom which followed a joyous feast when the scales told of an alarming loss of weight." (Courtesy of the Norwalk History Room at the Norwalk Public Library.)

Another way to cool off by the shore was to go camping at Calf Pasture Beach. This image is one of a series of camping photographs taken there in the early 1920s. To the left of this unidentified woman with a pail, beneath the striped canopy, is a hanging canvas bed. To her right is a comfortable looking striped folding chair. (Courtesy of Nancy Moore and her grandparents Linda Anna McMahon Smith and Elbert Jacob Smith.)

CALF PASTURE BEACH, NORWALK, CONN.

The first use of Calf Pasture for pasturage was in the 1650s. Today, Calf Pasture and Shady Beach are the largest public beach areas in the city and offer a full view of Long Island Sound and all of the Norwalk Islands. The large silver-colored binocular viewers there have been made by Tower Optical Company, Inc., of East Norwalk since 1933.

Linda and Elbert Smith relax and enjoy their pet cat on a camping trip at Calf Pasture Beach in the early 1920s. (Courtesy of Nancy Moore and her grandparents Linda Anna McMahon Smith and Elbert Jacob Smith.)

This home was that of Col. Thomas Fitch, who commanded a regiment of American troops around 1755 to Ticonderoga and Louisburg. The story has been that the popular ditty "Yankee Doodle" was written by British army surgeon Dr. Richard Shuckburgh in mockery of the varied dress Fitch's troops wore while stationed near Albany, which included feathers stuck in their hats by Fitch's sister, Elizabeth. The home was located on East Avenue near Hendricks Avenue, near today's Yankee Doodle Bridge on I-95. Note that there are some historians who believe this account to be untrue.

The advertisement for the Shore Haven Inn in the August 29, 1910, *Norwalk Hour* reads, "New this Season. Exceptional Cuisine. Ideal location on Long Island Sound . . . Table D'Hote Dinner Wednesday and Saturday Evenings $1.50." A fruitful spring exists nearby, behind Pine Hill and between Shorehaven Golf Course and the sound, which was a place treasured by the earliest settlers, and likely Indians before that, and also where boats came to have their firkins (water casks) filled.

In 1699, the first schoolhouse in Norwalk was built on East Avenue and was 18 by 20 feet with a door at one end and a fireplace at the other, a wide board floor, and benches without backs. This postcard shows an old schoolhouse, built 1826, that was also on East Avenue and was later moved to Mill Hill Park, where it is today.

When the city was consolidated in 1913, the Mayflower Fire Department retired its hand-drawn piece of apparatus and leaped into a new era with a shiny new red pumper truck built by the Barker truck company of South Norwalk. Mort Roberts was the first paid driver. (Courtesy of the Norwalk History Room at the Norwalk Public Library.)

The Founder's Stone Monument, located on East Avenue in front of the East Norwalk train station, marks the vicinity where the earliest homes were built. The monument was first located at East Avenue and Fitch Street and marked the original settlement and meetinghouse (which was at the corner of East Avenue and Fort Point Street) and was erected by the DAR in 1895. (Photograph by the author.)

Mathew Marvin was one of the earliest settlers. Community plots were located at Pine Hill, and the first planted crops were corn, wheat, rye, oats, and barley. During the Civil War, the Marvin family grew onions and sold them to the government at 42¢ a bushel. In the 1950s, the Taylor family donated the Shady Beach area. The 29-acre Marvin-Taylor Farm park area was purchased by the City of Norwalk in the 1970s for a park and school site.

IN MEMORY OF THE FIRST SETTLERS
OF NORWALK, 1649.

A SENSIBLE, SERVICEABLE AND A FORCIBLE PURPOSE FOLK

GEORGE ABBITT	DANIEL KELLOGGE
ROBERT BEACHAM	THOMAS LUPTON
STEPHEN BECKWITH	MATTHEW MARVIN, SEN.
JOHN BOWTON	MATTHEW MARVIN, JR.
MATTHEW CAMPFIELD	ISACKE MORE
NATHANIEL ELI	JONATHAN MARSH
THOMAS FITCH	WIDOW MORGAN
JOHN GRIGGORIE	RICHARD OLMSTED
SAMUEL HALES	NATHANIEL RICHARDS
THOMAS HALES	JOHN RUSKOE
WALTER HAITE	MATTHIAS SENTION, SEN.
NATHANIEL HAIES	MATTHIAS SENTION, JR.
REV. THOMAS HANFORD	MATTHEW SENTION
RICHARD HOMES	THOMAS SEAMER
RALPH KEILER	RICHARD WEBB
WALTER KEILER	

This monument is erected at the East Norwalk Historical Cemetery in memory of the first settlers of Norwalk in 1649. One of the oldest cemeteries in Norwalk, it is maintained by the Third Taxing District. Among the many notable people who have been buried here is Thomas Fitch IV, who was the 29th colonial governor of Connecticut from 1754 to 1766. His grave is a table tomb. The overall footprint of the cemetery was reduced in size when the trolleys first came through, as one corner of the property was lopped off to accommodate them down Gregory Boulevard. (Photograph by the author.)

Three

URBAN SOUTH NORWALK

The Old Well Hotel is pictured here. According to the *New York Herald* of February 2, 1874, there was a "Great Fire in South Norwalk . . . the most destructive fire which has visited this city since it had its organization . . . broke out in the harness room adjoining S.H. Hopkins' Livery Stable . . . great effort was made to save the stables and hotel . . . the saddest feature of it being the burning to death of sixteen horses. Colonel F.F. Stedman was the first to notice the fire and only succeeded in rousing his wife, family and guests from their slumbers in time to make good their escape . . . all was a mass of blackened ruins." Unfortunately, the proprietor had recently declined to renew his insurance because he claimed "rates were too high." (Courtesy of the Norwalk History Room at the Norwalk Public Library.)

An *Illustrated News* engraving depicts a morning express train traveling at a high rate of speed that went off the opened drawbridge into the Norwalk Harbor and steamboat *Pacific* on May 6, 1853. The engineer did not notice the signal, which resulted in 46 people being killed, many of whom were physicians returning from a medical convention. Among those who perished was jeweler Thaddeus Birke along with his cargo of $250,000 worth of diamonds, pearls, and gold jewelry. This was the very first train bridge disaster in the United States.

This wreck on February 11, 1890, occurred when New York, New Haven & Hartford Railroad engine No. 118 was pulling an eastbound freight train toward the drawbridge, which had just been opened to allow a boat to pass. A signal indicates the open draw, and a device called a derail protects trains by forcing a derailment well before the bridge. The engineer and fireman were able to jump clear before the train left the tracks and were only slightly hurt.

The corner of Washington Street is seen in this view looking toward South Main Street before the railroad bridge was built and the railroad tracks elevated. Once the tracks were elevated, the location of the station was moved from here to Monroe Street, where it sits today. The switch tower at right was moved across the street. (Courtesy of the Norwalk History Room at the Norwalk Public Library.)

A parade on Washington Street around 1900 passes by a very tall, narrow building on the right. Railroads used switch towers to control areas of track to prevent trains from crashing. A tower operator would send the correct signals and then throw levers that were connected to the tracks, thus changing the direction of the track. Today, the restored 1896 building is home to the Switch Tower Museum.

Hotel Mahackemo, South Norwalk, Conn.

Hotel Mahackemo was located on Washington Street and South Main Street, and was later named the Roger Ludlowe Hotel. It was in the area where the 50 Washington Street building is today. Emil Roth and Julius Goldschmidt established R&G Corsets in 1880 on North Water Street. As business grew, the factory was moved to 21 Ann Street by 1895. One thousand employees produced 7,800 corsets daily. The corset was an essential part of women's clothing at that time. A *Harper's Magazine* ad proclaims, "The new model 837 combines the good points of the straight front, low bust design, with sufficient length over the hip to conform with the present dress styles and yet remain easy and comfortable." The prices of corsets ranged from $1 to $10. (Below, courtesy of the Jewish Historical Society of Fairfield County.)

Washington Street is pictured with a trolley around 1910. Thanks to the determination of a few people and the creation of the Norwalk Preservation Trust, this area underwent a coordinated renovation in the late 1970s that improved the buildings and streetscape from their once blighted appearance to a clean, fresh look that is now Historic SoNo. This includes two of the few cast iron–front buildings still in existence in Connecticut. Today, Washington Street is known for its restaurants and unique stores.

Samuel Clemens (Mark Twain) was a frequent guest at the Clifford Hotel, which was located near the railroad station at the corner of South Main and Elizabeth Streets. In 1904, the hotel had 70 rooms, 30 baths, an elevator, and telephones. On February 24, 1923, firefighters fought the blaze here for 27 hours; the bitter temperatures caused the water to freeze as it left the hoses.

Trinity Episcopal Church was located at the foot of Flax Hill Road (then West Street) and West Avenue. Many people remember witnessing the horrific general alarm fire on July 21, 1974, with the exploding stained glass and the steeple that toppled over. Fortunately, none of the firefighters were hurt. The church was renovated in a different style, and the steeple was not rebuilt. Today is the Miracle Temple Church.

Written on the back of this postcard to Miss Gertrude de Cleeny of Peekskill, New York, is "this is a very pretty place, plenty of business. I like the place better than Stamford not so much hot air as Peekskill, knocking as usual, Jenine." Crescent Terrace was eliminated along with homes on Spring Street, now occupied by Dr. Martin Luther King Jr. Boulevard.

The Franklin Street School, earlier known as Union School, was built around 1854. An addition was made in 1897 and the building remodeled. Note that this is not the same school as the one on Flax Hill Road, which was Ben Franklin Junior High in later years. Today, this area is home to the Webster Street parking lot next to Norwalk's tallest building, 50 Washington Street.

The Central Fire Station was also located on Franklin Street. In 1913, neighbor Putnam Hose Company moved into this building. The Charles A. Volk–Central Fire Department Station was built on Connecticut Avenue to replace this firehouse in 1963. A new central firehouse was completed in 2013, and hanging in its atrium is the 1882 station bell from this building.

The First Congregational Church was financed by Algernon Beard in 1888 (the Beard Estate is on top of the hill at left). The Soldiers and Sailors Monument in front of it was dedicated in 1900 in memory of Grand Army of the Republic members. Beard was one of the city's first hatters and later was head of Norwalk Lock Company. In 1955, "a spectacular blaze destroyed the then 113 year old carriage house at 31 Flax Hill Road built in 1842," according to the *Norwalk Hour*, and on July 5, 1962, the home, which was abandoned, burned down. The only part remaining is its gazebo, which was moved to a site on Wilson Avenue overlooking Wilson Cove.

The Flax Hill Memorial is located at 7 Hillside Avenue (near Flax Hill Road and the rear entrance of the former Ben Franklin Middle School). British and Hessian troops came up the hill from Long Island Sound on July 12, 1779. An actual cannonball was found a hundred years later and is embedded into the monument, which was erected by the DAR in 1896. (Photograph by the author.)

West Washington Street is pictured around 1900. Emanuel Knishkowy writes in his recollections of growing up from the 1920s to 1950s, "On West Washington Street there were Puerto Ricans (mispronounced by my mother as Paprikans, since paprika was a familiar word), Norwegians, Irish, Jews from Europe, Italians, Germans. . . . The reasons for their getting along I believe were that they respected each others' differences, liked one another, and were good neighbors. It was like a small United Nations but with lots of good will. And in the middle of it all, symbolically, stood the Salvation Army, which cares for many of the world's poor. I hope we are as nice to each other today as people on West Washington Street were in those days. If not, maybe we have something to learn."

The C.L. Barker and Company factory started in 1899 and expanded in size until the buildings covered an acre of ground on Crescent Street. The company manufactured one- and two-ton trucks as well as firefighting vehicles. The trucks had solid rubber tires, a four-cylinder engine, and a worm-gear drive and had to be cranked. Barker also manufactured two-cycle marine engines as the Norwalk Launch Company at Pine Island. (Courtesy of Peter Bondi.)

A fleet of Rudolf Motor Lines trucks is parked behind one of the family homes at the corner of Day and Raymond Streets. Rudolf Motor Lines was owned and operated by David Rudolf and his family until 1958. All five of his sons worked for the company as soon as they could reach the pedals. (Courtesy of Steve Rudolf.)

The Palace Theatre is pictured with the facade it had when it was a vaudeville theater in the early 1920s. Mae West, Harry Houdini, and other major entertainers played there. Later, it was a movie theater. When the Hurricane of 1938 struck, Joseph Kilbourn recalled, "We piled into our 1936 Packard sedan . . . a double feature of *Dracula* and *Dr. Frankenstein's Monster* was playing, the picture kept dying because of periodic outages . . . we were told by the ushers the movie was cancelled and we had to leave."

Hoyt's Theatre is pictured in the early 1900s on Washington Street. Built in the 1870s by Mortimer Hoyt, it was later named the Rialto. In 1941, it was remodeled in an Art Deco style by interior decorators Riseman and Lercari under the personal direction of Warner Bros. designer Herman Maier. Due to declining attendance associated with the popularity of television, it closed around 1960. The outside of the building and its details can still be seen today. The inside is now condominiums and shops.

Morris Nevasky ran this grocery store on Railroad Avenue in 1926. Nevasky (right) was a Lithuanian immigrant. He and his wife Ethel's seventh and youngest son, Leo Nevas (left), worked in the store when he was younger. In later years, Leo was Paul Newman's attorney and helped launch Newman's Own and the Hole in the Wall Gang camps for children with life-threatening diseases. He was also an international human rights activist involved with Jewish causes. (Courtesy of the Jewish Historical Society of Fairfield County.)

This gentleman looks ready to ride solo on his Harley-Davidson motorcycle, as his sidecar is unhooked near his garage somewhere in South Norwalk. (Photograph by M. Manugian, courtesy of Ben Guerrero Collection.)

City Hotel, South Norwalk, Conn.

The former City Hotel and Music Hall, built in 1871, was located at 40 South Main Street. It was once a flophouse frequented by drug addicts and prostitutes, but the city acquired it by eminent domain in 1992 and sold it to the Human Services Council, which renovated the hotel portion into assisted living quarters. The renovation was in keeping with the SoNo revitalization, which focused on the preservation of the neighborhood's historic architecture.

This is the interior of the beautiful music hall that was on South Main Street. A crystal chandelier hangs from the center. A 1911 advertisement for the music hall lists a three-digit phone number, and one could buy tickets from the box office or at Weed's Drug Store. (Courtesy of the Norwalk History Room at the Norwalk Public Library.)

Harris and Gans Coal Company was founded in 1904 by Abraham Harris and his son-in-law, Edward Gans, on South Water Street. In the 1940s, Klaffs had a lumberyard on Water Street that sold "K-Houses"—complete housing packages that included building plans, lumber, electrical, and plumbing supplies. All the builder needed to supply was the labor. There was a great postwar demand for housing, and many of these homes are still in existence in Fairfield County. (Courtesy of the Jewish Historical Society of Fairfield County.)

The horse-drawn street-sprinkling cart and steel refuse collecting cart of the South Norwalk Street Department are pictured in 1909. As the roads were dirt at the time, the sprinkling of water and street oiling were necessary maintenance.

Emmanuel "Manny" Seligson and Sam Slobodkin are seen in Seligson's Cigar Store. Founded in 1925, the tobacco and candy store eventually became a large distributor of these products and was later sold to Pepsi-Cola. (Courtesy of the Jewish Historical Society of Fairfield County.)

South Norwalk Fire Department Company No. 1 was at 9 Haviland Street. The settlement was known as Old Well, as sailing ships in the olden days pulled up to docks along the inner harbor and waited their turns to fill up their water casks. The actual well is shown on the *Beers Atlas* map of 1867 east of Water Street and 75 feet south of Washington Street. In 1870, Old Well was incorporated as the City of South Norwalk.

In 1824, steamboat service began between Norwalk and New York City with the *John Marshall*, which was later replaced by the *Fairfield*. In the late 1800s, the *Adelphi* was commissioned to run service between the two cities. On September 28, 1878, the boiler exploded, and there were 30 fatalities in the Norwalk Harbor. The boat was rebuilt and renamed the *City of Albany* and put back into service. The accident was a consequence of the owners using an unsafe boiler. (Courtesy of the Norwalk History Room at the Norwalk Public Library.)

Multiple hat companies set up shops from the 18th century to the 1960s. Cavanaugh, Dobbs, Knapp Felt Hats, Knox, and Volk were some of the largest. At their height, hatting companies in Norwalk employed an estimated 35,000–40,000 people.

The historic Beth Israel Synagogue congregation built this Moorish Revival building in 1906 on the corner of South Main and Concord Streets. The design was influenced by that of the 1872 Central Synagogue in New York City, which also has onion domes. Today, this well-preserved wood-frame building is the location of the Canaan Institutional Baptist Church and is in the National Register of Historic Places. (Courtesy of the Norwalk History Room at the Norwalk Public Library.)

Columbus School used to be a neighborhood school. The statue of Christopher Columbus pictured here in front of the school is now located at the Heritage Wall on West Avenue, included with many tablets on the wall commemorating the many diverse groups that have settled in Norwalk. In 1982, this school, the first magnet school, became a pioneer in the effort to voluntarily desegregate the schools in Norwalk. There is a lottery system for entry into the Columbus Magnet School, and the school has won the Blue Ribbon of Excellence Award.

"Meet me at Woolworth's" was the slogan for the F.W. Woolworth's store on Washington Street. While it sold most everything under the sun, nothing was sold that cost over 5¢ to 10¢.

Norwalk Meat Market and DiLeo Drug Store were at 54–60 South Main Street on the corner of Elizabeth Street. The building looks much the same today and includes a grocery and a place to buy lottery tickets, send money, and prepare tax documents. Across the street is the new police headquarters, which opened in 2005. (Courtesy of the Jewish Historical Society of Fairfield County.)

Irving Hall owned the I. Hall Furniture Moving and Heavy Trucking Company, which specialized in long-distance moving. The expressman is shown here driving his Norwalk-made Barker truck. (Courtesy of the Norwalk History Room at the Norwalk Public Library.)

The South Norwalk train station at Washington Street and Railroad Avenue is pictured. This station was demolished and a new station was built on Monroe Street, where it remains today. (Courtesy of the Rowayton Historical Society.)

DR. WADSWORTH'S SANITARIUM, "WOODS COURT," SOUTH NORWALK, CONN.

In 1904, Alvin D. Wadsworth, MD, opened Dr. Wadsworth's Sanitarium. Also known as Woods Court, it is described in a 1906 advertisement as an institution "for the care and treatment of select cases of the various Nervous and Mental Diseases, such as Neurasthenia, Melancholia, Hysteria, Chorea, Epilepsy, Paralysis, Alcoholic and Drug Addictions." One of the most famous patients who stayed there was Allyn King, a Ziegfeld showgirl who ruined her health by taking "reducing pills" to keep her contractual obligation not to gain weight. She disappeared from the sanitarium after being there almost two years and went to stay with her aunt in Greenwich Village. There, in 1938, she committed suicide, leaping from a fifth-story window to the courtyard below. The concrete-and-brick building still exists today, square in the center of the public housing project on the hill in Monterey Village. Its red roof is visible from miles away.

VIEW OF LONG ISLAND SOUND FROM DR. WADSWORTH'S SANITARIUM, SOUTH NORWALK, CONN.

SOUTH NORWALK, CONN. R.R. STATION
AFTER THE BLIZZARD OF 1888

G.S. NORTH
SO. NORWALK.

A light snow on Sunday, March 11, 1888, turned into a very heavy snowfall that continued through the following day and shut down all means of transportation for several days until being dug out. These postcards of photographs taken by G.S. North show people out and about after the blizzard greeting the first train to arrive in South Norwalk (engineered by Elbridge S. Jennings).

FIRST TRAIN TO ARRIVE IN
SOUTH NORWALK, CONN.
AFTER THE BLIZZARD OF 1888

This photograph has handwritten notes on the back that indicate the old gardens and nursery (that sold property so that the new railroad station could be built there), and also the old Congregational church in this view. The railroad tracks are "at level" in this photograph, that is, before they were elevated. Due to a dangerous curve in the tracks, the trains would sound their whistles just before they got to this area, hence the name "Whistleville."

Brothers William and Jake opened Josem's Department Store around 1910 at Bouton and Lowe Streets. According to Marianne Josem, "It was a general store that had dry goods, clothing, sewing items as people made their own clothes. It thrived before there were automobiles and became a center of social activity. Immigrants from Russia, Eastern Europe, Germany, Hungary, Ireland and Italy would come when they first arrived in the states and bought big trunks that they would load up with clothes." (Courtesy of the Jewish Historical Society of Fairfield County.)

Above is a scene from *The Gypsy*, a Hungarian operetta. At one time, Norwalk had the second-largest Hungarian population in the United States. Many settled in the Whistleville area of the Springwood section of Norwalk. St. Ladislaus Church on the hill and the Hungarian Reformed Church carried on the traditions of the homeland. Italians were the next wave of immigrants to come into the Whistleville area at Lexington Avenue, Ely Avenue, and Bouton Street. They, too, were hardworking, just like their Hungarian neighbors, and shared a lot of the same family values. There were celebrations on the feast days of St. Ann, St. Mary Morgia, and St. Vincent. The photograph below depicts a 1951 clambake held on the picnic grounds of Santa Maria Della Morgia society on Lexington Avenue, unfortunately ended in a big raid by police for dice game gambling that was going on inside. (Above, courtesy of the Norwalk History Room at the Norwalk Public Library; below, courtesy of Peter Bondi.)

In 1893, a small tract of land owned by Rev. Robert B. Snowden was purchased by the Methodist Episcopal Church for $270. In 1931, there was a grand auction sale to sell off the rest of the Snowden Estate, partitioned into 173 separate building lots on Ely Avenue, Laura Street, and Lexington Avenue. The terms were 10 percent down, 10 percent due a few weeks later, and the balance paid in $5 monthly payments to Norwalk Savings Society. Later, in 1952, the adjacent area on the ridge above Ely Avenue was developed as a public housing project for 220 families and was named Samuel Roodner Court. The neighborhood has changed from the way Joseph Ruta remembers growing up in Whistleville, where his father had Ruta's grocery store and used to deliver vegetables in his Model T. The building on Lexington Avenue still has the name on it, but it is now remodeled into apartments.

There were many shops near Hotel Mahackemo along Railroad Avenue. The only structure that is in this scene that still exists today is the conical building in the far distance at right. That building is on the corner of North Main Street at Washington Street near today's railroad overpass bridge and was a brewery at the beginning of the 20th century.

Doris and Joe Blum's Family Grill is pictured around 1950. The diner was located at 71 North Main Street. (Courtesy of the Jewish Historical Society of Fairfield County.)

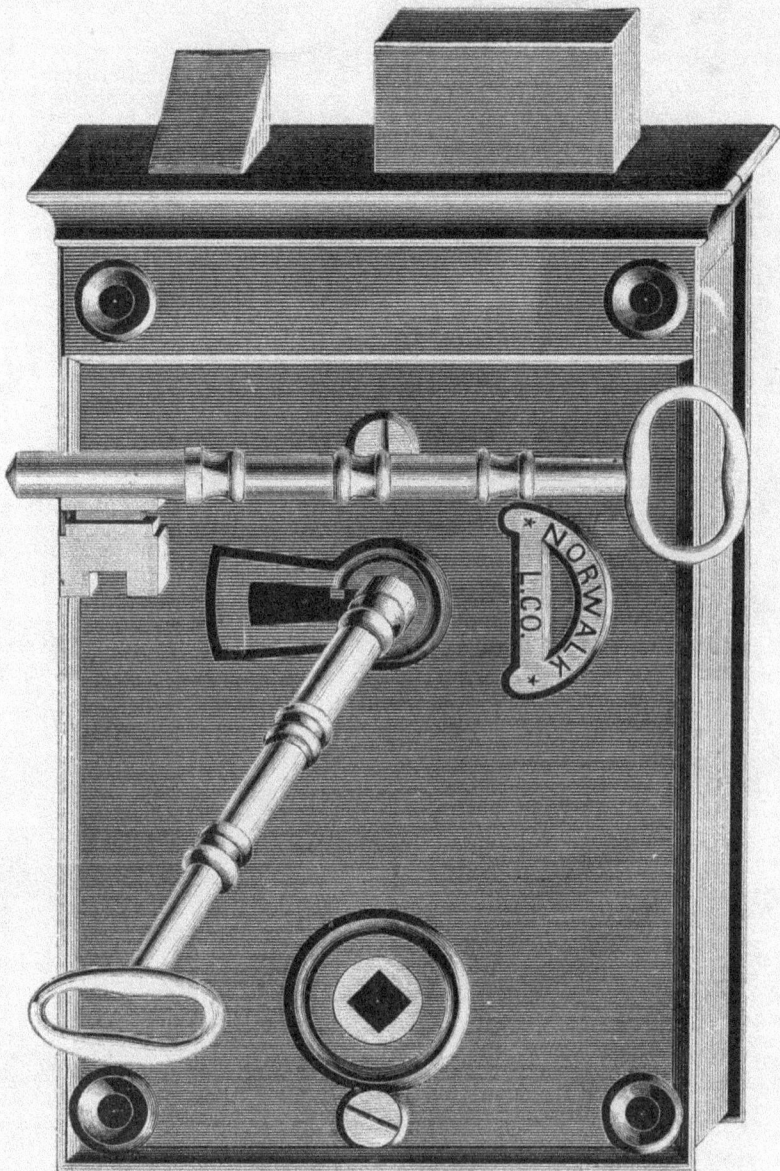

No. 1630.

TO CHANGE THE HAND.—PUSH THE HUB PARTLY THROUGH THE CASE, TURN THE BEVEL
THE HAND REQUIRED.

This catalog page is from the Norwalk Lock Company. Located on Water Street, the company was incorporated in 1856 and employed 500 people. The company produced locks and builder's hardware in iron, silver, brass, and bronze. Armaments for the Civil War, World War I, and World War II were produced here. The building was saved from demolition, preserved as creative office space, and contributed towards Norwalk's designation as a Preserve America Community in the federal government program.

Norwalk's second Carnegie library, the South Norwalk Public Library at 10 Washington Street, is a Greek Revival building constructed in 1913 with a $20,000 grant from the Carnegie Corporation. Carnegie provided funding for over 1,600 libraries across the country, and of the 11 in Connecticut, two are in Norwalk. This building is more typical of what was constructed and is in the National Register of Historic Places. It was renovated between 2004 and 2006.

In 1940, Louis Gardella of Gardella's trucking company purchased the old Seal Ship Oyster House on Water Street and named it Rex Marine. Soon after, along with Neal Lyons, Gardella opened up Lyons Pier Restaurant. Eventually it became just "the Pier." By the 1950s, Lyons got out of it, and E.C. Jones took over, with his assistant manager, a parrot named Jonesey that E.C. always walked around with on his shoulder.

In 1905, the Andrew Radel Oyster Company was organized, and its headquarters was located in South Norwalk. The company owned oyster beds from Maryland to Massachusetts. Andrew Radel was the largest oyster bed owner in the United States, and he owned and operated a fleet of 30 boats. (Courtesy of the Norwalk History Room at the Norwalk Public Library.)

Washington Street's 1867 bridge, which connects South Norwalk at the left to East Norwalk on the right, is in front of the Norwalk River Railroad bridge in this view from Norwalk Harbor. The present railroad bridge was built in 1896 by the Berlin Iron Bridge Company of East Berlin, Connecticut, and has a 562-foot span with rotating swing span 303 feet long. This bridge is one of only 13 bridges erected by the company in the state of Connecticut.

Four

THE ISLANDS
AND SHORELINE

Dutch navigator Adrian Block, while exploring the Connecticut shoreline in 1614, proclaimed the Norwalk Islands to be the Archipelago Islands. The Stewart B. McKinney National Wildlife Refuge encompasses 51 acres of Sheffield Island, Chimon (68 acres), Goose (4 acres), and Peach (3 acres) Islands as refuge for nesting birds such as herons, as well as a resting place for migratory birds. Also there is the native eastern prickly pear cactus, or *Opuntia humifusa*.

In 1860, John H. Keyser "spent thousands of dollars building a road across the marsh connecting the then Keyser Island with the mainland and converting the rocky island into a park, with rare trees, shrubs, and greenhouses surrounding a fine house," according to the *New England Magazine* in 1901. In the late 1800s, he sold the summer residence to a monastery known as Manresa's Institute, a retreat for Roman Catholic priests.

Boat Landing, Keyser Island, South Norwalk, Conn.

Jackson S. Schulz, attorney for the reformist Committee of Seventy, issued a statement that Keyser, a plumbing contractor with New York City, had admitted guilt and was turning over $650,000 in trust while awaiting the investigation. Keyser's mansion was one of the "Summer Palaces of the Ring" featured in the September 2, 1871, issue of *Harper's Weekly*. Keyser initially maintained his innocence, then handed over his books and became a witness against the Tammany Ring.

Thomas Nast's highly effective *Harper's Weekly* cartoons "would continue to aid the anti-Tammany crusade by such powerful weapons," according to the *New York Times*. This cartoon shows the adjoining shorefront estates that New York City's William "Boss Tweed" Marcy's four henchmen purchased at the mouth of the Norwalk River. The four included John H. Keyser, Elbert A. Woodward (who lived on Woodward Avenue), James Ingersoll, better known as "Ingersoll, the Tammany chair-maker," who lived at the top of Quintard Hill, and Andrew Garvey, who lived in the house pictured below, Judah's Island (now Shorefront Park). The area was named after Judah Gregory, who owned the property in the 17th century.

Capt. Nathan Roberts first built a house in 1848 on Pilot (Tavern) Island, which was rented to pilot Joseph Merrill. Elaine Deysenroth explained that, in 1904, her "great, great Uncle Ebenezer Hill then bought Tavern Island, that was known as Pilot Island." Ebenezer built the house and the caretaker's cottage, taking lumber over on the winter ice from the access on Bluff Avenue. Ebenezer also owned many adjacent oyster plantations. In 1938, Lillian Hellman wrote *Little Foxes* there. A 1922 advertisement shows both Pilot (Tavern) Island and the residence on Sheffield Island for sale. In 2012, Tavern Island was on the market for $12 million. The listing reads, "Private Island with year-round access via mainland property . . . main residence, caretaker's cottage . . . boat house with workshop, game room . . . separate tea house, in-ground pool, private beaches, protected harbor with dock." Norwalk property taxes are $166,000 a year for island and mainland access.

In 1804, Capt. Robert Sheffield purchased Sheffield Island. His son-in-law Gershom Smith bought it from him and put up a hotel in 1818. In 1827, Smith became the lighthouse keeper when the navigational beacon tower was erected on the island. The tower was replaced in 1868 by the current lighthouse, which was decommissioned in 1902. Peck Ledge and Green's Ledge replaced this as beacons to the Norwalk Harbor. The lighthouse is now a local landmark and museum run by the Norwalk Seaport Association. (Courtesy of Peter Bondi.)

Robert Corby, head chemist of Fleischmann's Yeast, purchased his estate in 1923 through public auction from Alfred Mestre on Sheffield Island to develop his Island Club. The property consisted of a stuccoed main house, another house known as "the Bungalow," gardens, and a roofed terrace. He used Tavern Island's dock next to Hickory Bluff for his two boats, *Rebel*, named after his wife, and *Betty B.*, a workboat named after his daughter. (Courtesy of Peter Bondi.)

Located on 46 acres at the eastern end of Sheffield Island, the Island Club consisted of a golf course, a landing for small airplanes, tennis courts, and stables with racing horses and polo ponies. It was a combination yacht, country, and beach club, and European royalty and well-known visitors were entertained there. Daily excursions would leave Gene's Boat Livery in Rowayton. The club closed down in 1937, mainly due to lack of fresh water, and in 1942, the estate suffered $7,000 worth of damage by vandals. Vandalism has always been a problem for island properties. Today, nothing is left of it but the stone pier, which can still be seen (in this view) to the left of the Sheffield Island lighthouse dock. (Both, courtesy of Peter Bondi.)

One of the advantages that Norwalk has had for the oystering business is the acres of islands in the harbor that provide good shelter to oyster beds. Norwalk oysterman Capt. Peter Decker, founder of the Peter Decker Oyster Company, was the first in the industry to introduce steam power for the purpose of towing and hauling oyster dredges in 1874. When he converted his sloop, *Early Bird*, into a steamer, he said, "the rest of the oystermen laughed at me and said I was a fool; but after they found that I could catch more oysters than they could, they went to legislature and had a law passed to prohibit steam dredging in natural beds." Soon thereafter, a state law was passed that limited steam-powered oyster dredging to only two days a week. (Both, courtesy of Peter Bondi.)

Written on the back of this 1908 real-photo postcard sent to New Zealand is the following: "This picture of our launch taken last August. It is at anchor just below our house. I thought you would like to have one. Do you care for photo views? If so I hope to send you some this summer as I have a camera and hope to get a few good ones out of it, Remmie Gardiner 35 Cove Avenue, East Norwalk."

In 1876, Charles Smith, descendant of the founder of Smithtown, Long Island, came to Norwalk to start an oyster business and purchased Hoyt's Island (near Village Creek). His children used a shell walk to get to school. In 1889, he purchased 12 acres by the creek off Woodward Avenue named Smithville and divided it into parcels on what are now Burwell, Sable, and Yost Streets. (Courtesy of Peter Bondi.)

Incorporated in 1905, the Harbor View community originally consisted of summer cottages with part-time residents. In the 1950s, there was a shift to year-round homes, and today, it contains 109 homes. As Harbor View was once an island named Daskam Island, after the mariner Capt. Samuel Daskam, there used to be a bridge that ran from Neptune Avenue to get there. A heavy truck, weighted down with stones from the construction of the Manresa power plant in the 1950s, caused part of the bridge to collapse. Instead of repairing the bridge, it was torn down, and the power plant built up the causeway several feet higher for resident access. There are tennis courts and a clubhouse with a beach that can be used by its residents.

Woodward Avenue was named after Elbert Woodward, who was president of the Fairfield County Fire Insurance Company, one of the four companies that paid on losses sustained in the Great Chicago Fire of 1871.

At the beginning of the 20th century, the Meadows had an expansive view and was not yet developed. Driving down Meadow Street today, its hard to imagine this view now that used auto parts, scrap metal recycling, and other industries block this view to Village Creek and Long Island Sound.

In 1910, baseball games were played here on an athletic field known as Amusement Park on Meadow Street. When the circus came to town, it pitched its big tent here. This photograph is of Floyd and Howard King, owners of the Gentry Bros. Circus, which is setting up for its circus in 1929. Another circus that set up there was the Cole Brothers Circus.

A homecoming picnic was held on the grounds of Baxter Park on Woodward Avenue for returning veterans of World War I in 1919. (Courtesy of the Norwalk History Room at the Norwalk Public Library.)

This aerial view shows LaJoie's Auto Wrecking. Ahead of his time in recycling, Frank LaJoie started his LaJoie's All Waste Materials in 1933 on Meadow Street. He invented his own paper baler, which compacted mixed paper mostly obtained from the Hat Corporation of America on Van Zant Street. As a child, his son Don LaJoie would collect paper from the sidewalks in front of the stores in South Norwalk. Frank invented a special hammer for removing tires off of trucks quickly. Don used this when he raced cars at Danbury Racarena. Later, Don added a hammer mill shredder that would also separate out the copper, aluminum, brass, and pieces of tire from the rest of the automobile metals. Respectful of his neighbors, Don would never run this on washday Monday. (Courtesy of Don LaJoie.)

The Village Creek area is pictured before development. Homes built in this area in the 1940s made up Norwalk's first planned interracial community. The Community Cooperative Nursery School had its start in the basement of one of its homes before moving to its present site on Old Trolley Court in Rowayton.

Women stroll back from lunch at Nash Engineering around 1920. Nash Engineering was founded in 1905 as a manufacturer of liquid vacuum ring pumps and compressors. In 1918, three floors were added. As early as 1780, this site was the location of the earliest of the potteries, Hoyt Pottery, located at "the Village," where many pottery shards of redware and blackware were discovered in old dump heaps in 1933. (Courtesy of Michael Shaffer.)

Five

TRANSFORMATION
OF WILSON POINT

The steamer *D.R. Martin* awaits New York passengers at Wilson's Point around 1890. During the Revolution, this area was known as Horn and Hoof Creek, so called because stolen cattle were slaughtered here by Tory raiders and useless parts dumped into the water before the enemy rowed to Long Island.

A carryall (horse with a large carriage) would pick up passengers from the trolley line and bring them to the clubhouse at the Knob. (Courtesy of the Norwalk History Room at the Norwalk Public Library.)

The *City of Albany* steamer docks at what was known in the 1890s as Wilson's Point pier. The manipulative Lewis O. Wilson had approached farmer Isaac Belden about purchasing the (then) Belden's Neck. Isaac had other plans for the land he inherited from his father and wanted to give each of his daughters a share. In 1825, Wilson married Belden's daughter Harriet and thus acquired her share of Belden's Neck. By 1835, there were steamboats leaving there. (Courtesy of the Rowayton Historical Society.)

The Norwalk Yacht Club was originally an elegant Victorian building constructed in 1895 on Bluff Avenue, seen near Hickory Bluff. Gilbert Bogart was its first commodore. The railroad and shipping facilities of the Housatonic Railroad, as in this photograph of 1890, would have been the view from that location. In 1963, the club relocated across the harbor to this area in Wilson Point, where it is today. (Courtesy of the Rowayton Historical Society.)

The Wilson Point station was erected by the Danbury & Norwalk Railroad. Pipes ran to the oil tanks of nearby Standard Oil Company. One of the railroad's most important functions was to transport milk to the Manhattan markets—there were even two runs made on the Sabbath to achieve this. The low-sided gondolas in this 1882 photograph were loaded with coal and headed inland to fuel dealers. (Courtesy of the Norwalk History Room at the Norwalk Public Library.)

Many large English Tudor estates, resembling castles and featuring turrets, are located in Wilson Point. During construction in the 1920s, Native American gravesites were located on Woodland and Valley Roads. In 1926, three more skeletons were discovered in graves six feet deep lined with clam and oyster shells. New York architect Frank J. Forster designed this home for Charles Wesley Dunn, Esq., who wrote the federal government's Pure Food and Drug Act.

"Wednesday afternoon at the Knob" features a group of women gathered and relaxing on a rocky bluff overlooking the Long Island Sound. Twice a month, the Ladies Whist Club would meet for cards and talk. The Knob Outing Club had private bathhouses, a casino, two tennis courts, and an ice cream pavilion open eight months out of the year. There were dances held there on Saturday nights. Started in 1891, the Knob's membership increased to 200 swimmers, divers, and tennis players. The club ended by 1920. The building was razed during the Great Depression, and several years later, a new house was built on its foundation.

During World War I, railroad operations and shipboard activities made Wilson Point a major freight terminus. In 1881, the railroad added boat service to nearby Bell Island as the Hickory Bluff bridge was not built yet and access was only by water. A hotbed of activity during Prohibition with bootleggers and rumrunners, Wilson Cove was the site of one of the biggest illegal alcohol hauls of all time. (Courtesy of the Rowayton Historical Society.)

When the United States entered World War I, the US Shipping Board leased the southwestern end of Wilson Point from the Burchard Estate and had armed men at the entrances and barbed wire surrounding the property. There was also a warehouse, storage shed, and barracks erected as the site was used as a naval storage base. At the end of the war, there was an auction held to sell off all the surplus property. (Courtesy of the Randalls.)

Six

THE VILLAGE OF ROWAYTON

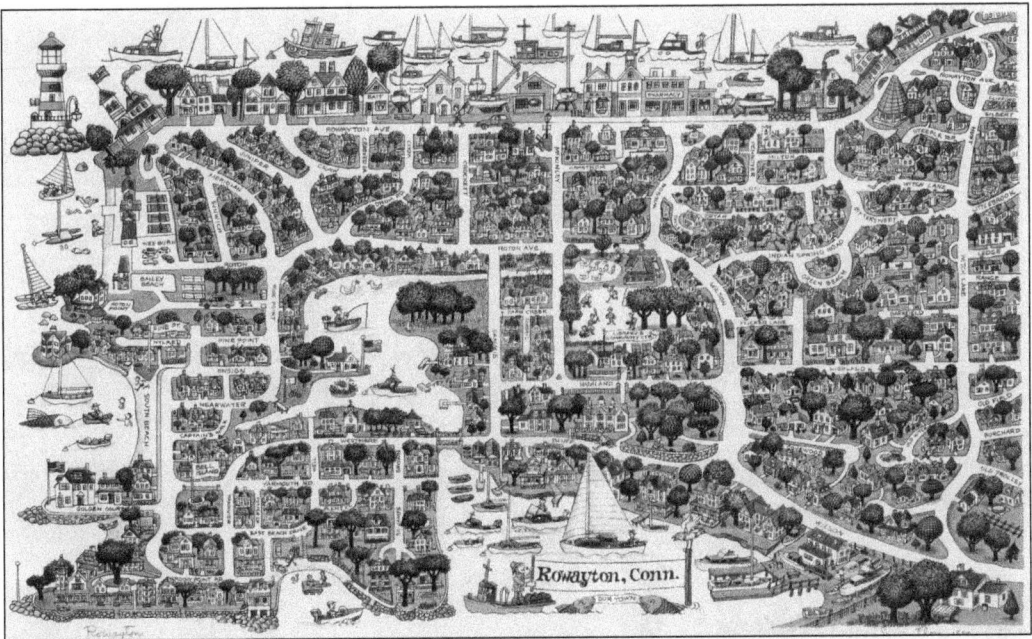

"Rowayton is a village at the mouth of the Five Mile River, whose chief industrial interest is oyster growing. Artists find it very paintable with its wharves and watercraft and picturesque location. John Kensett painted some of his best pictures . . . near Rowayton" was written in 1901 by Angeline Scott, and much of the same could be said today. (Map of Rowayton by artist Jim Flora, courtesy of Joel Flora.)

This wooden suspension bridge was built in the 1890s to carry people over the Five Mile River from Darien. The mill is on the corner with Raymond Street in that town. Tokeneke Road was a cart path along the trolley tracks that was gated off until 1915, when it opened as a road to accommodate the increase in automobiles. An arched stone bridge replaced the wooden one from 1912 until 2010. (Courtesy of the Rowayton Historical Society.)

Emily Stevens wrote on the back of this 1887 photograph, "*Kate C. Stevens* largest of the three oyster steamers of the Stevens Oyster Company . . . at the 'Upper Dock.'" This dock property was filled, dredged, bulkheaded, and enlarged to accommodate the three steamers around 1890. (Courtesy of the Rowayton Historical Society.)

By the late 1800s, thirty-five oyster companies operated out of the Five Mile River. Captains built homes along "Oysterman's Row" on Rowayton Avenue. By 1879, Rowayton and South Norwalk earned the title "Oyster Capital of the World." By 1924, Rowayton marshes were filled in with material dredged from the river by real estate developer Ralph Case and offered for sale as the Rowayton Beach Association (on the left). His father and grandfather were once oystermen.

Pictured is the living room at Rock Ledge, the Highland Avenue estate of James A. Farrell, president of US Steel Corporation and founder of the Farrell Steamship Lines. The property consisted of an Elizabethan-style house, a gatehouse, a horse barn, a carriage house, and several outbuildings. Just five years after its completion, the house burned to the ground after a fire broke out during a wedding reception. It was rebuilt in granite the same year. (Courtesy of George Middleton.)

A trolley stops at "Beehive Corner," which is the name for the curve in Rowayton Avenue just north of Witch Lane. In the distance is the old Baptist church that was torn down to make way for the United Church of Rowayton in 1966. (Courtesy of the Rowayton Historical Society.)

The stained-glass windows from the old Baptist church are kept safe down in the basement of the new church. The United Church of Rowayton building that replaced the Baptist church has a unique design with a somewhat spiral-shaped roof similar to a conch shell (or some say a billowing sail) designed by architect Joseph Salerno in 1962. Too large for local roads, some of the longest wooden supports of the new church needed to travel the old Housatonic Railroad line to Rowayton in 1963.

The property that is now known as Pinkney Park was first referred to in Norwalk town records as "the Shipyard" and was nothing more than a piece of common property to build and launch a boat. The Seeley-Dibble-Pinkney house was built around 1820 and possibly includes part of the shipyard building, as a portion of the basement floor contains ballast left over from the overseas shipping trade. Above is a c. 1870 photograph with oyster boats in the Five Mile River at left. The Sixth Taxing District's purchase of the property from the Pinkney family in 1971 occurred after years of persuasion by Doug Bora Sr.—it was going to be left to a church in Brooklyn, New York, and thankfully he convinced them otherwise. Today, it is the site of the Rowayton Historical Society as well as the grounds for many events such as the annual River Ramble, Sunday concerts, and Shakespeare on the Sound productions. (Both, courtesy of the Rowayton Historical Society.)

This building, today the Rowayton Market, is the longest-running continually operational market in Connecticut. Brothers Samuel and James Richards first purchased the property in 1753 as a general store. Alfred Seeley owned it from 1823 to 1878. The photograph above was taken around 1900, when it was Seeley's son-in-law Alphonso Dibble's grocery and dry goods store. The image below shows the interior of the store. (Both, courtesy of the Rowayton Historical Society.)

The Five Mile River Depot opened in 1868 and was renamed Grantville following a town vote. Twenty-five years later, the name was changed to Rowayton. This is the New Haven Railroad pumping station around 1900 at the dam at Boylston (now Chasmar's) Pond, which was needed for the steam trains to take water as they passed by. (Courtesy of the Rowayton Historical Society.)

The inscription on the back of this c. 1910 photograph reads: "Taken . . . at White's Farm near the strawberry patch where for many years Rowayton children gathered about 5 am to pick berries at 2 cents a quart. At height of season, fast pickers would earn $1.00 before going to school. In season, strawberries were followed by raspberries and then blackberries . . . was on high knoll at corner of Wilson and Roton Avenue." (Courtesy of the Rowayton Historical Society.)

This Miller and Baker roller coaster at Roton Point Park was built in 1934 and was named Skylark. The "safety chain dog" or safety ratchet was patented by John A. Miller. Its design prohibited the car from rolling down the incline and also gave it the distinctive clinkety-clank sound that is made while trains on wooden coasters are going up. (Photograph by Albert Stelkovics, courtesy of Walter Stelkovis.)

These people are ready for a swim in their woolen bathing suits at Roton Point on August 21, 1914. In the background is the lifesaving station, and off to the back left is where people would get their souvenir photographs taken. Visitors could rent a bathing suit there if they did not bring one. The rented suits had belts with "RP" buckles. (Courtesy of the Rowayton Historical Society.)

From the top of one of the Roton Point roller coaster peaks, one can see the striped roof of the loading and unloading platform (now Bayley Beach picnic pavilion) and merry-go-round building at water's edge on the right. The amusement park's last season was 1941, when steamships—and men (and women)—were needed for World War II. (Photograph by Albert Stelkovics, courtesy of Walter Stelkovis.)

The Sixth Taxing District purchased one part of the park as a public beach. It was named Bayley Beach after Neville Bayley, who first managed, then owned Roton Point Park. The former roller coaster building had a flat roof added as a floor for picnic tables, and with an added snack bar, lifeguard shack, changing rooms, and bathrooms, it is used as the pavilion to this day. (Photograph by Emma Smith, courtesy of David Smith.)

This little building once stood at 135 Rowayton Avenue, first as a shoemaker's shop and then as a war relief shop. It is featured in a November 1918 edition of *Women's Home Companion* in an article entitled "A Lilliputian War Shop." Local ladies would sell food, doilies, and arts and crafts to raise money during World War I to support war orphans at a US hospital in France. The building was relocated to Pine Point Road across from the entrance road to Bayley Beach and Roton Point. (Courtesy of the Rowayton Historical Society.)

A favorite place for children to ride their bikes to, Louie's had a wide selection of candy and magazines and was located on the corner of Rowayton Avenue and McKinley Street from 1945. The same location years before was called "Guider's Corner." Guider's hardware store was located there and supplied the oyster boats with hardware. It also had a blacksmith shop in the back. (Courtesy of Lloyd Rex Gatten.)

The Thomas School was founded by Mabel Thomas in 1922 on Bluff Avenue. Here, Diana Barrymore (left) makes her acting debut in a Christmas pageant at the Thomas School, where she was a boarding student. Like her renowned actor father, John Barrymore, she went on to be an actor and made her Broadway debut. Sadly, she lived a life of drugs, alcohol, depression, and negative publicity and died from an overdose in 1960 at age 38.

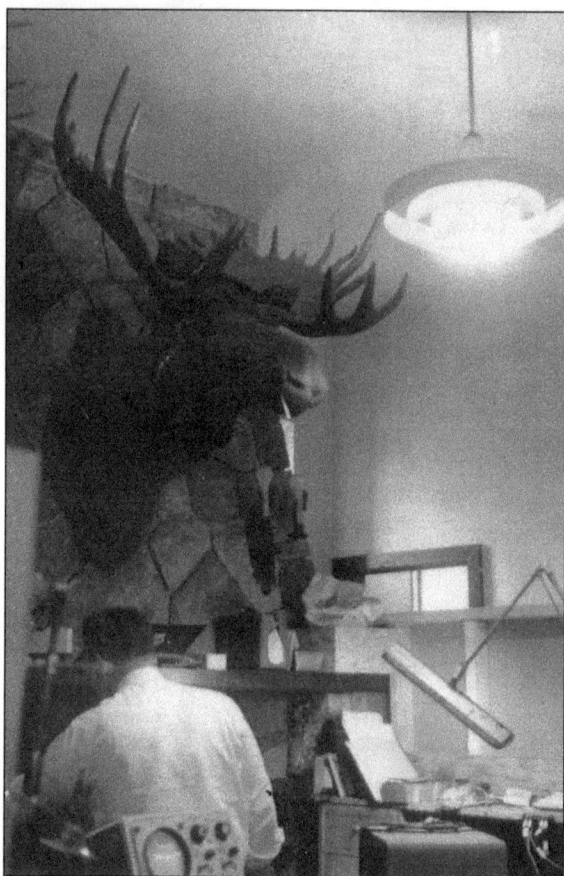

The world's first business computer, the Univac Model 409 prototype, was unveiled in 1951 to a gathering of military and government officials in the former Farrell Estate carriage house and stables. James Rand, founder and president of Remington Rand, used "the Barn" for research on its top secret project between 1947 and 1951 and hired prominent engineers to work there. Gen. Douglas MacArthur was chairman of the board of Remington Rand during this period. The company shipped its first business computer to the Internal Revenue Service in 1952. The building was later sold to the Sixth Taxing District for use as the Rowayton Community Center and Rowayton Library. The moose head is still over the fireplace, and a red bulb is added to his nose at Christmas. The grounds are now used by the public for paddle tennis and dog walking, and the Rowayton Gardeners maintain the gardens and the newly refreshed greenhouse and potting shed. (Both, courtesy of the Rowayton Historical Society.)

Seven

BROOKSIDE AND
WEST NORWALK

"It was also voted and agreed, August 26, 1666, that such men . . . as doe goe to cutt hay on the other side five mile river, the towne will stand by them in the action to defend them . . . and if they shall be afronted by Stamford men, the towne will . . . prosecute them by law," according to Norwalk public land records. Pictured in this view facing west toward the red mill is Flax Hill Road around 1900. Flax was grown for the local production of linen and rope and was also exported to the British Isles. (Courtesy of the Rowayton Historical Society.)

John and Clara Fodor bought their farm in the 1880s. Loretta Noonan Aboelnaga, who lived at Fodor Farm, remembers, "It was definitely a working farm. They sold milk, eggs, and lambs . . . the field in the back was for hay or pasture for animals . . . and a huge [vegetable] garden." Now owned by the city, the old farmhouse at 328 Flax Hill Road is undergoing renovation. There are 350 garden plots, a pavilion, an orchard, and a tree farm. (Courtesy of the Fodor family.)

The Old Brookside School, seen around 1910, was earlier known as the Middle Five Mile River School. The South Five Mile River School was in Rowayton, and the North Five Mile River School was in West Norwalk. These schools were under the jurisdiction of the Darien School Society in the early 1800s but were taken over by Norwalk when the State of Connecticut abolished school societies in 1856. (Courtesy of the Norwalk History Room at the Norwalk Public Library.)

Traendly Greenhouses, started by Frank H. Traendly at the beginning of the 20th century, was located in Brookside on Rowayton Avenue and also on Raymond Street in Darien. At one time, it was the largest grower of roses and orchids in the eastern United States. Many laborers who worked there were from the Whistleville area of Norwalk. The boilers needed constant coal shovelers as well as deliveries by horse-drawn wagons to keep the temperature constant. (Courtesy of Larry Scharbach.)

Brien McMahon High School was built in 1960 on Highland Avenue. James O'Brien McMahon was appointed US assistant attorney general in 1935. Famous cases included prosecuting John Dillinger's lawyer for harboring a criminal, trials associated with "Baby Face" Nelson, and the Harlan Coal Miners case, which upheld the right of labor to enforce unions. In 1945, McMahon was chairman of the Senate Special Committee on Atomic Energy, and his McMahon Bill that calls for controlled scientific research was signed into law as the Atomic Energy Act of 1946. (Courtesy of the Norwalk History Room at the Norwalk Public Library.)

In 1880, Joseph Cox of Roton Hill (now Highland Avenue) built a Victorian home with a tower. Fine artist Harry Stacey Benton was the architect who transformed this into an English Tudor home in the early 1920s, and the home was featured in advertising for the Atlas Portland Cement Company. Benton's artist studio was at the end of Topping Lane, where he created illustrations for magazines, including the popular 1917 advertisement "Ain't We Cute Cream of Wheat Kids?" featuring Rastus. (Courtesy of Jordan and Lisa Grant.)

West Norwalk was a very rural area. The meetinghouse on West Norwalk Road was built in 1868 and was originally used as a chapel by four Protestant churches. It has been restored by the West Norwalk Association as a community gathering space.

Old MacDonald's Farm was located on the Norwalk-Darien Town Line on Connecticut Avenue from 1955 through 1979. Owned by John and Helen Schulten, it consisted of a restaurant, a general store, a candy shop, a bakery, and a large petting zoo and amusement park. There were plenty of animals to see at Old MacDonald's Farm: monkeys, llamas, sheep, buffalo, and in this stable goats one could pet. In 1957, a baby elephant named Shakuntala arrived—she was a gift to the children of Darien from their pen pals in Mercara, India. She ended up going to the Beardsley Zoo in Bridgeport when she got too big and hard to handle. Another baby elephant named Lollipop later replaced her in the 1960s. (Both, courtesy of George Nemeth Jr.)

The penny candy store was a favorite—red hots, rock candy, candy dots, and more could all be had here once children made their selections through the glass cabinet. The restaurant was well known for its hamburgers and its rustic barn feel—the booths had feed cages in the corners like horse stables and there was sawdust on the floor and antiques all about. There was a player piano, an old viewer, and a big waterwheel outside. (Courtesy of George Nemeth Jr.)

One of the favorite rides at Old MacDonald's Farm was the antique cars with the center rail—riders really felt as though they were driving the cars. There was also a swan boat ride, a train that went around the park, an 1886 Parker carousel with wooden horses, and a fire engine hayride. (Courtesy of Ben Guerrero Collection.)

Old MacDonald's Farm was a favorite place for birthday parties; one could also go to the driving range or miniature golf course next door and then Carvel ice cream. The lion drinking fountain was always a hit. After the park closed, the drinking fountain went from Old MacDonald's Farm to Stew Leonard's. An identical fountain exists outside a store at 149 Madison Avenue in New York City. (Courtesy of Ben Guerrero Collection.)

The dark brown footbridge to Old MacDonald's Farm over the Five Mile River is the only part that still exists today located near the large River Park building that was erected on its site. There always seemed to be ducks, swans, or geese in the small pond nearby that the children loved to feed. (Courtesy of George Nemeth Jr.)

The Norwalk Drive-In had its grand opening in 1951 with the movie *Follow the Sun*. Admission was 65¢ for adults, and children under 12 were admitted free. "Brilliant Screen, Finest R.C.A. Sound, Hard Paved Surface, Tiled Sanitary Rest Rooms, plus Technicolor featurette and two color cartoons on every program" were advertised. The Kiddies Playground was a real hit for the children and had swings and a giant metal circle that spun called a Big Spinner (also called the Merry-Go-Round). Kids would come dressed in pajamas and once the movie started get on the roofs of their cars in their sleeping bags and blankets. The dancing snack figures were the trigger to head to the concession before affixing the speaker to the car window. In the background of the photograph below is the newly built public housing project Colonial Village. (Both, courtesy of the Scicchitano family.)

High winds with gusts of 70 miles per hour in April 1970 toppled the 95-by-65-foot movie screen. The wooden frame was rebuilt in steel. The Norwalk Drive-In continued until 1979 when it was sold for $2 million to make way for a Kmart shopping center. (Courtesy of the Scicchitano family.)

In 1904, St. Mary's Seminary, generally known as "Ferndale" because of the abundance of ferns on the property, had this location on Weed Avenue as a seminary to train priests, known as Holy Ghost Fathers. The community has always been able to walk the grounds, and its paths, one of which is near the pond, have the 12 Stations of the Cross. Today, it is a hotel and convention center.

Hungarian immigrants work on fur pelts in the trimming plant at Royal G. Millard's in West Norwalk. The 1901 *Norwalk City Directory* lists this as a hatter's fur manufacturing plant. (Courtesy of the Norwalk History Room at the Norwalk Public Library.)

Lou Renzuella's Uncle Al started the original Swanky Franks in 1949 on the Post Road. Al said what made the place special was that it "not only served quality hot dogs but made each of his customers feel like part of the family." The large yellow letters that used to be mounted on the roof came off during a storm in 1982. (Photograph by the author.)

Eight

WINNIPAUK AND CRANBURY

The Merritt Parkway was proposed by Congressman Schuyler Merritt as a Depression-era public works project to alleviate traffic off the Post Road. With its vistas and landscaping, the parkway was planned to be scenic as well as functional. George Dunkelberger designed many of its unique bridges and tollbooths. Connecticut's first cloverleaf exits and entrances are at the interchange with Route 7 in Norwalk. Completed in 1940, it is one of the few roads listed in the National Register of Historic Places.

Dresden Lace Works, Norwalk, Conn.

Dresden Lace Works was a lace manufacturing plant incorporated in 1910 that made "art linen" or Cluny lace (lace sold to primarily American corset manufacturers). The business was sold at auction in 1918 to Richard Mueller, who acted as an alien property custodian. During World War I, German companies were considered dangerous. It was later renamed Connecticut Lace Works. Artist studio workspaces, a wholesale florist, and other industries are today located in the beautiful old factory building.

Mill Pond and Bridge.   Norwalk, Conn.

The mills in the distance are no longer in existence, as all of this area is now on land occupied by the Route 7 connector. This is a view of the Norwalk River where it takes a bend looking from Riverside Avenue, which is in the foreground (near where Casatelli Marble is today). At the time, the bridge connected over to Forest Street, which met with Fair Street. The mills are on the land that is now a big parking lot for a medical building near the Cross Street Bridge.

From the 1830s until 1865, a wealthy Norwalker, Phebe Comstock, funded the Norwalk Mills Company expansion. Her aunt of the same name (1731–1817) was the owner of the last slave held in Connecticut, the white-haired Onesimus, because he had refused his freedom. For 50 years, he never missed a Sunday in his pew at Norwalk Congregational Church, riding there with her. He declared himself a "voluntary slave" in the census of 1850.

Several mills dotted the area on this side of Main Avenue. The gristmill was one of the first on the Norwalk River. The arched stone bridge in this postcard still exists today, hidden underneath another bridge on Grist Mill Road between the end of the Route 7 connector and Main Avenue near the Connecticut Department of Motor Vehicles.

Jazz pianist Horace Silver of Norwalk writes in his autobiography, *Let's Get to the Nitty Gritty*, "My father worked at the Norwalk Tire Company, a factory that made automobile tires and rubber soles for shoes. He was in charge of a small department that made rubber cement. Dad spoke with a slight accent, but he spoke good English. . . . There were a few other Cape Verdeans who lived in South Norwalk, namely, Nick Santos, the barber, who played music with my dad; and Mr. Perry, who managed a poolroom and also played music with my dad. You might say they were pretty enterprising in the black community." Above is a Norwalk Tire advertising photograph showing how strong the tubes are. Norwalk Tire and Rubber Company was founded in 1914 in the former Lounsbury and Bissell Manufacturing building in Winnipauk. Below is a Norwalk Tire and Rubber Company employees photograph. (Below, courtesy of Peter Bondi.)

Cranbury Chapel and the Old Cranbury School are two parts of the hamlet of Cranbury. Originally known as Cranberry Plains, this area at the intersection of Newtown Avenue and Chestnut Hill Road had cranberry bogs at one time. Gregory's Store was opened in 1884 and was razed in the 1960s. Broad River, Brookside, and West Norwalk are other areas in Norwalk considered hamlets since each had at one time a school, a church, and a store with undefined boundaries as part of a larger town. (Both, courtesy of the Norwalk History Room at the Norwalk Public Library.)

The Melton Museum of Antique Automobiles was located on an eight-acre site on Route 7 half a mile from the Merritt Parkway. "America's Favorite Tenor" James Melton, a well-known singer from the 1920s to 1950s who appeared in concerts, movies, radio, television, and the Metropolitan Opera, was also an avid car collector who owned over 100 automobiles. He negotiated with the State of Connecticut in 1941 to build a tourist attraction. His plan was that if the state would pay $50,000 to build the museum, he would donate the cars. Although the onset of World War II put that project on hold, Melton persevered on his own, and on July 14, 1948, he opened the 20,000-square-foot museum with 55 cars, antique bicycles, auto accessories, toy trains, and music boxes. Twelve hundred people, including official New York City greeter Grover Whalen (who forgot to bring the special scissors for the ribbon-cutting) and other celebrities, came the first day, and there were 1,600 paying customers on the second day. Admission to the museum was 60¢. (Both, courtesy of Margo Melton Nutt.)

The oldest car in the Melton Museum was an 1893 custom steam stagecoach, and the most modern car in the museum was a custom-built Detroit Electric. There was also a 1911 Mercedes of Vanderbilt Cup Race fame, a 1900 Rockwell Hansom Cab (the first New York City taxi), and a 12-passenger 1915 Stanley Steamer Mountain Wagon that had been used in Yellowstone National Park for sightseeing tours. In the front of the museum, there was a 1902 trolley car. There was a restaurant called the Stirrup Cup that served a variety of meals, including seafood, and also had dancing every Saturday. On the top of the building with the Melton Museum sign were brightly colored cutouts of some of the cars that were included in the collection. According to Melton's daughter, "He sincerely believed that everyone was as interested in the history of the automobile as he was. He felt that preserving the cars was only half the story, they should be shown to the public as examples of man's ingenuity and as the beautiful antiques they were." (Both, courtesy of Margo Melton Nutt.)

Edward Beach Gallaher built this 21-room fieldstone mansion on the property of the former Kensett Sanitarium, which burned down in 1912. He used the same architect and stonework as was used at St. Paul's Church on the Norwalk Green. The manor home features oak paneling, french doors, and stained- and painted-glass windows. Gallaher was owner of Clover Manufacturing Company on Main Street, maker of industrial abrasives. He is famous for building the Keystone Quadrocycle, one of the first horseless carriages, as well as marine engines. (Photograph by the author.)

Jenning's Slitting Mill and sawmill were on the Winnipauk Millpond on the Norwalk River in the 1790s. Dams provided the power for rolling mills that forged sheets of high-grade iron ore and slitting mills that produced nails and hoes. Later, the *Beers Atlas of 1867* shows an icehouse in this location, and today, it is occupied by the Merritt 7 complex of buildings. (Courtesy of the Norwalk History Room at the Norwalk Public Library.)

Nine

The Charm
of Silvermine

Silvermine is part of Norwalk but also includes a small part of New Canaan and Wilton. Legend has it that the c. 1690 silver mine was located on the east side of Comstock Hill Road near where it crosses with Silvermine Avenue and close to the Silvermine Brook. A former gristmill, the Silvermine Tavern, was built in 1811 and served as an inn and restaurant for many years. The area became a widespread settlement for artists, sculptors, and writers.

Popular baritone and Broadway performer Greek Evans and his wife, Henriette Wakefield Evans, had a dream of "bringing professional opera to Norwalk in a beautiful outdoor setting under the stars." This dream was realized as the Theatre in the Woods, which was a stone amphitheater that they built on their 40-acre farm on Oakwood Court. Pillars on Belden Hill Road marked the entrance to the 5,000-seat outdoor theater. The opening production on July 16, 1932, was *Robin Hood*, and Gov. Wilbur Cross and other important politicians were there.

Henriette Wakefield Evans was a world-renowned opera singer and star of the Metropolitan Opera in New York City. She and her husband, Greek Evans, performed and produced operas, musicals, and theater at the Theatre in the Woods from 1932 until 1937. The end came when the local musician's union pressured them to not hire New York musicians, and this eventually forced the Evanses to close the theater. The property was then subdivided, and homes were built. At one time, one of them had the former orchestra pit converted into a swimming pool.

The Saddle Ridge Riders are pictured at an unknown date. According to the *Norwalk Hour* of December 20, 1948, "the Saddle Ridge Riders entertained during the afternoon with musical selections" at the Christmas party for the Norwalk Aerie Fraternal Order of Eagles.

The artist and creator of Raggedy Ann, the rag doll with red yarn hair, triangle nose, and "I Love You" heart printed on her chest, lived in Silvermine for a time. Johnny Gruelle was born in Illinois in 1880 but moved to the East Coast in 1910 to become a freelance illustrator. He began writing the Raggedy Ann stories for his daughter Marcella, who was sick. The patent for the doll was secured in 1915, and in 1918, the *Raggedy Ann Stories* were published. Raggedy Andy, her brother in a sailor suit and hat, came out in 1920 and was first manufactured in Norwalk. Gruelle continued to publish one book a year. Marcella sadly died at age 13 of what authorities said was a heart condition, although her parents believed it was the smallpox vaccination. Gruelle began an anti-vaccination movement using Raggedy Ann as a symbol. (Courtesy of Joni Gruelle Wanamaker.)

Solon Borglum's barn was the gathering place for many artists. Attracted by the area's charming mills and winding roads and rivers, they settled here in the early 20th century and formed an artists' colony. In 1906, the Silvermine Guild of Artists was formed, and among the many fine artists were painters, cartoonists, graphic designers, and the opera singer Lily Pons. The photograph below was taken inside the barn at a fundraising event in September 2012 that reunited the works of many of the Knockers Club artists, who used to gather and critique each other's work. Borglum was a famous sculptural artist who was also part of a talented family—his brother, Gutzon Borglum of Stamford, carved the Mount Rushmore monument. (Above, courtesy of Silvermine Arts Center; below, photograph by the author.)

Visit us at
arcadiapublishing.com

www.ingramcontent.com/pod-product-compliance
Lightning Source LLC
Chambersburg PA
CBHW050708110426
42813CB00007B/2124